BK 15421
Acc. No. _____ Class No
MID-CHESHIRE COLLEGE
HARTFORD, CHESHIRE
Order No. 10695

This book is to be returned on or before
the last date stamped below.

BK15421

DENNIS

AND THE MIND GREW FINGERS

OPPENHEIM

SELECTED WORKS 1967-90

By ALANNA HEISS

With an Essay by THOMAS McEVILLEY

The Institute for Contemporary Art,
P.S. 1 Museum, New York
in association with
Harry N. Abrams, Inc., Publishers, New York

A PROPOSAL FOR UNDERSTANDING THE WORK OF DENNIS OPPENHEIM
Alanna Heiss

When I came to New York from the Midwest in 1966, I wanted to work with painters and sculptors and get involved with museum exhibitions. I hung around Max's Kansas City Restaurant—a watering hole for creative people—and went to artists' studios.

Early on, I heard about Dennis Oppenheim, and what I heard didn't quite make sense. His Land and Body Art pieces were seductive, and in the best sense of the word, his work was perverse. I'd see him across rooms, in bars and restaurants, but he seemed unapproachable. We never really connected.

At the time I listened to discussions among artists about Minimalism. Having studied logic and philosophy, I had some basis for understanding Conceptual sculpture. People like Robert Smithson made a lot of sense to me, but people like Dennis Oppenheim seemed to have a screw loose somewhere. His work just didn't fall into any system I was familiar with.

I went to London for a while, and when I returned to New York in 1970, America was the landscape of the Manson murders, the moon landing, and the Vietnam War. I knew I had to connect what was going on in American art with these national events, and Dennis Oppenheim seemed like the right connection. My desire to meet him became more intense, since I'd heard a lot more about him in Europe where he was widely regarded as an important artist.

A phone call to Dennis was rewarded with an invitation to dinner. He lived in Brooklyn, which was unusual at the time, and he lived a conventional life—a wife, children, one couch or more, a dining room. First I was shocked, then I felt comfortable, then I felt happy. Finally I was frightened. Clearly the man was out of his mind. There he was living in conventional circumstances, but his mind was someplace else. I was to learn that Dennis's capability for schizophrenia was exceptional.

After our first meeting—and I do not remember what we talked about—I followed every show he did. I was determined to see how his mind paralleled the development of my world. When I began to think I was understanding what was going on, I wanted Dennis there to suggest another lock, another key, another door that needed to be pushed open.

Dennis's work was in the first art project I organized in 1971 on the pier at the base of the Brooklyn Bridge. When it comes to working with him, my experience as an organizer and curator have always been positive: he's on time, is organized, civil, and communicative. He does what he says he'll do. The only problem—if you want to call it a problem—is that he pushes every exhibition he undertakes to the most extreme position possible.

For almost eight years I've been thinking about this exhibition and publication. And I've been thinking about Dennis. I've concluded that if there are people from other planets, it's probable that Dennis is one of them, an alien. Look at the facts: to begin with his work, the changes in his work, his mind, his attitude, and even his appearance would be a lot easier to explain if he were an alien, working from an experience that's different from ours. The information he takes in is different, and what he puts out seems to come from another data base, one that has been gracefully adjusted to ours.

Dennis talks a lot about dreams, and dreams may be his way of explaining to us humans where his ideas come from. When we think of visionaries, we think of earthly ones, people who have their feet on the ground, but look far out into the unknown. Dennis has never had his feet on the ground; they've always been in the air. That's why he made Earth Art. Think about how many of his pieces involve views from high up. And he has no fear of flying or falling. When NASA was talking about sending an artist into space, Dennis made it clear to everyone that he wanted to be the first.

Dennis clearly has a mission. It is one that is not easy for us to comprehend, largely because we expect missions to make sense. Dennis is not interested in making sense in the short run; he is more intent on expanding our vision, helping us see many levels of reality. He's optimistic about human beings, about what they're up to, about what they are capable of.

Making a work of art is essential to Dennis, and he will survive any stress to make art. No trend, no art world pressure, no gallery will make him change his direction or cater to an audience, because he cannot justify limiting his work to conform with what it means to be an artist. It's an essential, core conviction, even though he knows there are easier ways to do what he does. It's this determination to explore complex areas of human experience with a consuming conviction that makes us confident his exploration is valid.

Immortality is one of the perks of being an artist, that and long vacations. Dennis has even given up one of those perks—immortality—a fact that anyone who makes ephemeral art must face. Dennis expends tremendous energy on a piece—machines that will be taken apart, earthworks that will disappear. He spends precious resources on experimental pieces that are never sold and often cannot be maintained. He, by choice, squanders his chance for immortality. But it's all he can do. It is how he lives his life.

Dennis was a pioneer of Conceptual Art, a 1970s art movement out of which much of the art in the 1980s is derived. It is interesting to watch him return in his latest work, which is populist on a bizarre level, to that same field of daisies to pick some flowers. It's wonderful to see him working with the concerns of younger artists—installation ideas, science fiction, media, and environmental issues. If you consider the twenty-five year career he has had as an artist on this planet, you can see how he's made decisions that only young people make. The word conscience comes to mind. His ability to experiment makes Dennis a very young artist, with a very old mind. Today's young artists should take heed of his commitment to experimentation. He has a lot of wisdom to share since he's been around the block several times.

People say that Dennis's earthworks and machine pieces are uncollectible. But the problem of collectibility is actually one of possessibility. Ephemeral art shares this problem with most paintings, the possession of which is impossible for the ordinary person. Painting, like Dennis's work, exists only in memory, the memory of the visit to the museum, or the memory of the visit to the site aided by a photographic reproduction. In fact, it is somewhat easier to remember the works of Barnett Newman. Since so many of Newman's paintings are similar, and usually faithfully reproduced, you can see one and imagine others. They become lodged in one's visual memory. It's hard to do the same with Dennis's work; it changes too much and too frequently. And in many cases all that is left is a drawing or a scruffy, mysterious photograph of what was an exciting installation. When a work exists only in casual photographic form, it is difficult to revive the initial energy and excitement you felt standing there as Dennis flew overhead in a plane, crawled up a gravel pit, or warded off a tarantula creeping toward him.

The Oppenheim exhibition, *And the Mind Grew Fingers*, is an attempt to conjure up the original energy we experienced in the 1970s, to see if it is still alive today and what it might mean to a new generation. The publication brings together a coherent stream of Dennis's finest work—from his Earth and Body Art to his performances and installations, *Factories* and *Fireworks* series, and recent sculptures. The publication and exhibition are intended for young people, many of whom will get a chance for the first time to examine of the integrity of the 1970s, the authenticity of the effort, and the excitement of the product that came from artists for whom art was life. Mostly though, I hope everyone who visits the exhibition or reads the publication will understand and appreciate the wackiness of Dennis Oppenheim's vision.

THE RIGHTNESS OF WRONGNESS:
MODERNISM AND ITS ALTER-EGO IN THE WORK OF DENNIS OPPENHEIM
Thomas McEvilley

Designating An early series that has come to serve, somewhat arbitrarily, as the beginning of Dennis Oppenheim's oeuvre is *Sitemarkers*, from 1967 (pp. 8-9). Oppenheim would choose a site, usually on Long Island in New York, where he was working at the time as a junior high school art teacher. He would photograph the site and document its location, assign it a number, and then manufacture an aluminum stake with a number on it corresponding to the number of the site. The physical artwork consisted of a transparent plastic cylinder containing the photograph and the documentation of the site and a fitted sack containing the stake. The work, while simple in physical presence, is complex as a site marker for the location of the art process at that volatile moment in both art history and history in general.

In 1914 Marcel Duchamp initiated the practice of regarding something as art not because it was made with the intention of being art, but because it was somehow designated or contextualized as art, although it had been made for some different purpose. Duchamp would take an everyday object, such as a snow shovel, sign it, and exhibit it in an art context. As these works became accepted into art history they exerted a powerful subversive influence. In time the prevailing ideas about the nature of the art object and the art-making activity were revolutionized. This did not, however, happen at once. Duchamp's legacy did not bear fruit for about two generations. During that time, the eras of the schools of Paris and New York, the traditional Romantic view of the artwork as an aesthetic object created by an inspired genius, such as Pablo Picasso or Jackson Pollock, was more or less unquestioned. Duchamp's snow shovel lay, as it were, among the forgotten stuff in the attic, waiting to be rediscovered.

The rediscovery happened around 1960. By that time many had come to feel uneasy with the highly aestheticized art of the schools of Paris and New York. The winds of social change were in the air on a global scale with the advent of decolonization and the emergence of the so-called Third World, and the very survival of the earth was seemingly in question in the midst of the cold war, superpower politics, and endgame weaponry. In this atmosphere the works of Pollock, Mark Rothko, and others, while undeniably great in their way, had come to seem disturbingly precious, otherworldly, and removed from the real issues of life. In a world tossed by a tumult of cognitive reevaluations, from the Cultural Revolution in China to the Black Panther movement in Oakland, the bestowing of aesthetic pleasure in and by itself seemed less a contribution to reality than a distraction from it. This feeling gave rise to a succession of "movements"—Pop Art, Minimal Art, Conceptual Art, Earth Art, Body Art, and others—designed to locate the artwork somehow in the reality of life, not merely aesthetic reality, but cognitive and social realities as well. This was the moment when Duchamp's anti-aesthetic gestures became widely known. In 1959 Robert Lebel's book on Duchamp appeared, and in 1963 the Pasadena Art Museum mounted a retrospective of his work with an influential catalog. Duchamp's practice of creation by designation offered itself as a useful instrument for blurring the distinction between art and life. Artists began devising new methods for designation in addition to Duchamp's methods of signature and context.

In 1960 the French artist Yves Klein began to designate existing objects as his artworks by painting them with his patented pigment, "International Klein Blue." The Italian artist Piero Manzoni designated objects and persons as art by placing them on a sculpture pedestal (the *Magic Base*). Ben Vautier would issue "Certificates of Authenticity" designating some person or thing as his artwork.

In America the practice of designation came to be particularly associated with the ethical imperative of the site. Aesthetic art had separated itself from the life-world inside the sheltered environments of museums and galleries. The site was, on the contrary, a location in the real, outside world. As a real-life object could be designated an artwork, so a real-world place could be designated an art context. For many artists of this generation the idea of the site

(continued on page 10)

Sitemarkers with Information, 1967. Milled and anodized aluminum, photodocuments with photography and text. 1″ × 2″ × 9½″ markers, 14″ × 23″ photodocuments.

   Ten sites are selected and photographed. Ten aluminum markers are made and engraved with a number corresponding to each site. The marker and corresponding photodocument, which includes the photograph and a description of the site, are exhibited. Originally rolled into a plastic cylinder, the photodocument later was hung on the wall above the marker.

Opposite page, left: Site #5; *right:* Site #10.

became a new dogma, a value emerging from a reversed hierarchy. The museum or gallery had once functioned as a sacred or sheltered space, setting the artwork off from the surrounding world; now the fact of a work being embedded in a real world location was to be of its essence. There were complications, however, in dealing with career necessities such as gallery exhibitions.

In a series of works begun in 1968 called *Nonsites*, to indicate their somewhat reluctant capitulation to the gallery principle, Robert Smithson brought heaps of rocks into galleries and exhibited them along with photographs of the sites they had been taken from. Oppenheim's *Sitemarkers* belong

Overleaf: Indentations—Removals, **1968-69. Locations in New York, Paris and Amsterdam.**

Objects (usually debris) are selected in various locations. The act of removing these objects makes the impression of the removal evident on the land.

Proposals for Gallery Space, **1967. Blue line drawing. 16″ × 24″.**

The proposals involved limited walking corridors, tilted floors, and angled ceilings. From an original pencil on paper drawing (1967), a blueprint is made (1972). "I remember not wanting to do drawings, because I didn't want evidence of a hand and a pencil. I would run drawings through a blueprint machine, which removed any direct evidence." (D.O.)

in this context, and indeed are in the forefront of it for the first generation of American Conceptual artists. The documents and the surveyor's stake connected to the site by its number could stand in for the site in a gallery. The *Sitemarkers* effectively clouded the traditional distinctions between the artwork and the utilitarian object, and between the art context and the outside world.

Reversing Oppenheim's *Sitemarkers* were followed by his *Viewing Stations*, 1967 (p. 11). As the *Sitemarkers* reversed the relationship of art and world (from separation to an ambiguous union), the *Viewing Stations* reversed the relationship of subject and object, or of viewing and viewed. These artworks are not things to be looked at but places to look from—small platforms on which a single person could stand to gaze upon the world. From being an aesthetic object to be activated through contemplation out of context of the outside world, the artwork became a device to encourage insight into that world. The *Viewing Stations* also look like sculpture pedestals—they are not unlike Manzoni's *Magic Base*—and function similarly. Not only do they define the art-

(continued on page 16)

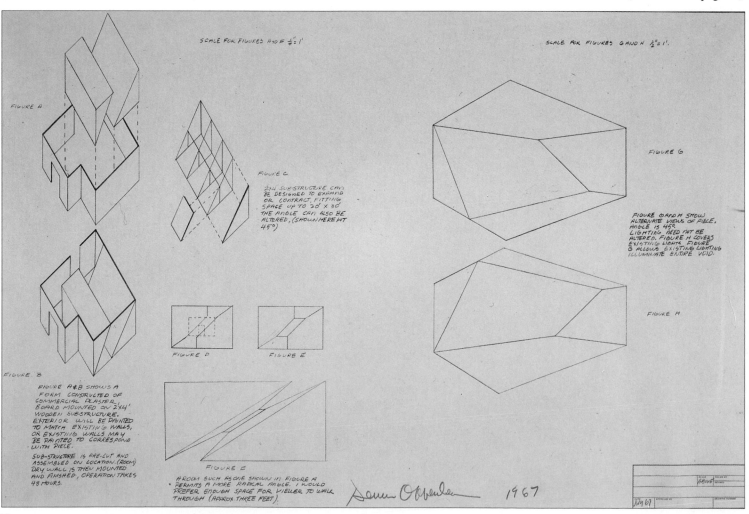

Viewing Station #1, 1967. Wood construction.
12′ × 15′ × 15′.

   In a gallery installation, the viewing
station is a platform that reverses the
viewer's relationship to an art object.
The art object becomes a platform to
view from, rather than an object to
be looked at. Also intended for
outdoors locations where the
platforms, or structures, can
be used for viewing land.

Gallery Decomposition, 1968. Scale model:
wood, cement, plaster. 18″ × 24″ × 30″.
   Construction materials consist of a substance (i.e., plaster) and a catalyst (i.e., water)
that are combined to form an architecture.
Here, the gallery is de-architecturalized in
the sense that the materials used in the construction are shown without the catalyst
(i.e., water).

work as a means with which to view the real world, they also treat the viewer and his or her act of viewing as the subject matter of the work; the act of beholding is itself what is beheld. It is with these pieces that Oppenheim's work begins to acquire its special emphasis on epistemology, or mental process, which would increasingly characterize it for the next few years.

A third series of works from 1967-68 that was involved in redirecting the art energy and setting new and broader parameters for the art experience was the *Indentations* (pp. 12-13). Oppenheim would find an object that had lain in the dirt in a vacant lot (in New York City, Amsterdam, or Paris) and would remove it, leaving the indentation of its own shape in the dirt.[1] The site would be photographed both before and after the removal. The indentation, that is, the absence rather than the presence of an object, was the artwork. In the rejection of Modernist aesthetics, with its obsession with the object, the idea of art as a removal rather than an addition was also being pursued in both Europe and America. Klein had given an exhibition in 1962 that consisted of removing the paintings from a gallery in the Museum of the City of Paris. Other artists, both European and American, were engaged in related gestures. Rather than adding yet another object to the already crowded world, the artist would begin to clear things away, on the analogy of clearing away illusions.

In America this tendency was associated in an ironic way with the fading authority of Clement Greenberg, the most influential of the aesthetic critics, who had advocated reducing the artwork to its absolute essentials. Minimal Art, starting in the early 1960s, had subversively carried Greenberg's reductive program beyond his intention by attempting to eliminate aesthetic elements as well as non-aesthetic ones; Conceptualism eliminated the physical process and even at times the object itself, in what came to be known (in a parody of the idea of Spirit which underlay the Greenbergian imperative) as the "dematerialization of art."

The themes of dematerialization, removal, and the anti-object informed another series of works from 1968 called *Decompositions* (pp. 14-15). In these works Oppenheim heaped the gallery floor with a powdered version of the materials of which its walls were made, such as sawdust or powdered gypsum.

Here the artwork is seen both as a physical demolition of the gallery itself—an attack on its ideology of preciousness and separateness, dissolving its walls to let in the outside world—and as a means of reversing the traditional aesthetic process wherein raw material is made into coherent form. Here art functioned as a way of undoing what had been unnecessarily done, a force that dissolved form back into the shapeless stuff from whence it came.

The Earth In 1968 Earth Art was born in the works of Oppenheim and a group of other young artists, such as Michael Heizer, Walter De Maria, Robert Smithson, and others. Most of these artists were recently out of art school and inspired by the sense of multiplying options in the air. Earth Art was a multifaceted strategy to redirect the art energy. On the one hand, it located the artwork in the real world of the landscape—indeed, often it made the landscape the work, but not in the sense of the Romantic reverence for scenery: it could be a scene of urban decay and desolation, or a strip-mined area that was brought into the expanded realm of art. In this sense, Earth Art, like other tendencies of the time, was about demystifying art by taking it out of its sheltered milieu into the world. On the other hand, for some of its practitioners Earth Art had certain ancient resonances, harking back to the era of megaliths, pyramids, and other monumentally scaled sacred objects sited in the landscape. In this somewhat contrary sense it sought to regain a pre-Modern feeling of the extra-aesthetic sacredness of art through a change of scale and location. Oppenheim's work was more of the first type than the second, but it had a theoretical focus that was different from either: it involved dispassionately working out certain principles that related primarily to a quasi-scientific methodology for art making, rather than to aesthetics, ideas of sanctity, or the project of demystification.

Oppenheim's *Landslide*, 1968 (pp. 18-19), executed off exit 52 of the Long Island Expressway, was one of the first earthworks that was actually realized rather than merely contemplated or sketched out; it was used by both *Time* and *Life* magazines in that year to indicate the beginning of the trend. Almost didactic in its dispassionate approach, *Landslide* involved angled boards arranged around a slope. It extended the idea of Minimal sculpture into nature with suggestions of longitude and latitude lines, while simultaneously evoking the idea of a bleacher or a communal viewing platform. Oppenheim thought of it as "activating" a preexisting area of the world. Insofar as an area of the world would be changed into an art area by this activation, the beginnings of "Systems Art," named by Jack Burnham in the 1968 *Artforum* article "Real Systems Art," can be seen. (Systems Art operates by transferring an object or site from one semantic system to another.)

In the spring of 1968 Oppenheim worked furiously at these theoretical proposals, defining the parameters of the emerging genre of Earth Art as he went along. *Directed Seeding*, (p. 34) 1969, was a wheat field harvested along lines pre-set by the artist in an oversize parody of Action Painting and painterly composition in general. In *Annual Rings* (pp. 24-25), the pattern of growth rings from a tree trunk was transferred to a huge scale and etched into the snow-covered ice of a waterway occupying the United States-Canada border and crossing a time zone line. Oppenheim's tactic of reconceiving something by radically altering its scale (usually by enlarging it) was emerging in these pieces, as well as his tendency to emphasize borders—temporal, spatial, behavioural—the breaching of them, the exchange of systems and contexts, and so on. In *Contour Lines Scribed in Swamp Grass*, 1968 (p. 23), a pattern of elevation lines from a topographical map was transferred to a swampy field that lacked the indicated elevation and would be submerged under water at certain times; the cartographer's sign was shifted both in scale and in meaning.

The rules that emerged for these works involved a found or real world element, such as the map lines, as an ethical surrogate for the site. Oppenheim, like other classical Conceptualists, felt constrained to work by preconceived extra-aesthetic rules that go back in form to Duchamp's quasi-scientific instructions for *3 Standard Stoppages* in 1913-14.[2] Among other things, this served to deny the traditional aesthetic view of art as an absolutely free play of intuitions—a view that seemed somewhat irresponsible in its disregard for external realities. The Romantic-Modernist belief that art was opposed to science was annulled by the introduction of scientific elements into the vocabulary. At the same time art was to be relocated culturally in an area of practical

rather than dreamy endeavor. What was emerging as a guiding principle in Oppenheim's work was a requirement that any element be justified by some external or found index; the lines, for example, of *Annual Rings* or *Contour Lines* could not be drawn freehand by the artist out of an expressive impulse; tree rings, map signs, or whatever, they had to have some real world, semantic context from which they were being appropriated into the "creative," or re-contextualizing, act.

Sometimes the real world index apppears flexible and somewhat subjective. In *Salt Flat*, 1968 (pp. 29-31), Oppenheim spread rock salt over a rectangular area of earth on Sixth Avenue in Manhattan; the size of the area was dictated by the amount of the material he could afford to buy. The arbitrary, real world index that served as limit for the piece was the money in his pocket. For the most part, however, the method remained linked to a kind of objectivity outside of the artist while carrying forward the issues of the moment, such as the critique of the relation between the gallery and the outside world. In the *Gallery Transplants* (p. 32), for example, Oppenheim took the dimensions of a gallery, then marked off a similarly bounded space outdoors. A cognitive reversal is involved; the real world index ironically was derived from the gallery, and then transposed to the outside world as a rejection of the reality of the gallery. Structurally, Smithson's *Non-sites* are similar in mediating the ideological opposition between the autonomous artwork isolated in the gallery and the engaged artwork sited in the outside world. The *Non-sites* are simpler, however, than the *Gallery Transplants* in that they do not involve the ironic reversal.

Another transplant piece, done for the first Earth Art show, which was organized by Willoughby Sharp for the Cornell University gallery in 1969, further complicated the method. Oppenheim redrew the boundary lines of the gallery in the snow of a bird sanctuary nearby. The gallery space transplanted into nature was then randomly activated by flocks of birds alighting on it in different compositions that were unaffected by the artist's intentions.[3] The piece involved another important anti-Modernist rule or tendency that was being articulated in the works as they emerged. The Modernist aesthetic view of art promulgated a myth of the complete control exercised by the artist—in whose work, for example, it was

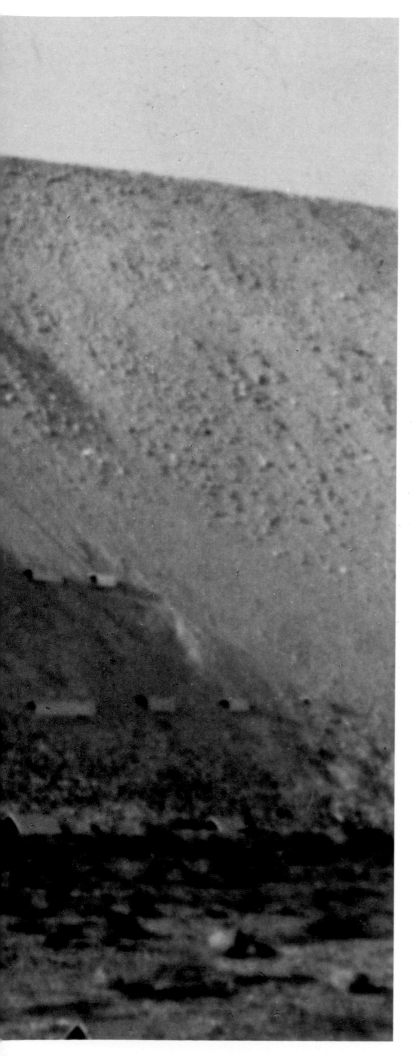

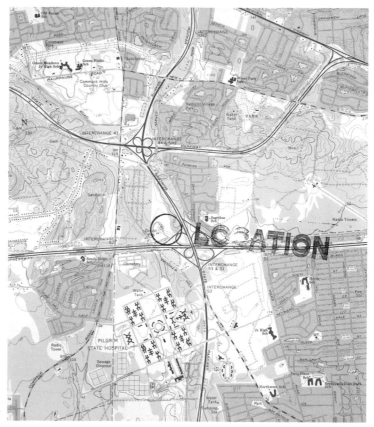

Left: Landslide, 1968. Exit 52, Long Island Expressway, Long Island, New York. Right angled boards, earth. 1000′. *This page, top:* U.S. Geological Survey, topographic map of the location; *bottom:* U.S. Geological Survey, aerial map of the location.

An abandoned gravel pit is activated by the placement of parallel boards against the 1000′ slope. The parallel bands are spaced at distances of two times the distance of the previous row, and look like latitude lines on a globe.

supposedly impossible to change anything without losing aesthetic integrity. Duchamp had articulated the counterprinciple, that of allowing chance to decide parts of the work (again in *3 Standard Stoppages*), and that part of his artistic legacy was also bearing fruit now. In Oppenheim's Cornell gallery transplant, for example, the intervention of flights of birds was an element outside the artist's control. Increasingly Oppenheim would come to feel that the artist should create the circumstances for an artwork to occur in—or set going the chain of causes which would produce it—but not the work itself, which remains hidden or unknown till it appears out of the manipulated causal web. The concept resembles the Modernist idea of the artwork as something self-created or miraculous, but reverses the power hierarchy. In the Modernist discourse the artwork, though in a sense self-created, still sprang somehow from the artist as medium; in this approach the artwork springs from the world as medium, the artist being more distanced.

Various works of the period investigated siting the art event within the agricultural and climatic time cycles of nature. The *Gallery Transplant* in the bird sanctuary, for example, was done in the winter and disappeared when the snow melted. It was like a part of nature in other words, and passed with the changing of the seasons. In *One Hour Run*, 1968 (p. 26), Oppenheim parodied Action Painting by cutting snowmobile tracks intuitively or expressively in the snow for one hour. Such pieces flaunted both their ephemerality and their conditionality, operating against the Modernist crypto-religious belief in the artwork as eternal and autonomous like a Platonic Idea. The work is subject to the conditions of nature like everything else, in opposition to Modernist work, which was conceived as outside of nature and not susceptible to its rhythms of change and decay.

Oppenheim's work is characterized not only by the kind of clear analytical seeing of theoretical issues that is found, for example, in Smithson's work of the period too, but also by a tendency to complexify methods of presentation through structural reversals. In *Cancelled Crop*, 1969 (p. 35), a crop was harvested in the shape of an X and the harvested wheat was kept from processing and never consumed. A cultural sign, the X of cancellation, has been applied to a field of wheat as it might be applied to another sign on a sheet of paper. Culture has coopted nature. The retention of the wheat from processing and consumption is again symbolically a subversion of aestheticism—a denial that the raw material of life needs reshaping as art and presenting to an audience. So nature re-engulfs culture again, but on culture's terms. There is little hint of the flower child mood of affirmation of nature as a solution to the problems of culture.

For Oppenheim, the commitment to the earth as a site was part of a more general commitment to the site. Other sited pieces located the artwork in urban rather than rural matrices. In *Sound Enclosed Land Area*, 1969, four tape recorders were buried in cages at four points in Paris, delineating a rectangle of 500 by 800 meters. Each tape loop projected a voice repeating its respective cardinal point: North, South, East, or West. Here the solipsistic emphasis of much early conceptual art was stressed. Joseph Kosuth's work showing a chair and a photograph of the chair, or William Anastasi's picture of a wall hung on the same wall, and other works of the era, are related. In something of the spirit of Frank Stella's famous remark about Minimal paintings, "What you see is what you get," works like these tend to emphasize the self-identicalness of the real world elements of the piece, in opposition to the Modernist idea of the alchemical transformation of real world elements by the art-making process.

Turning Around Oppenheim's oeuvre as a whole is characterized by a long, slow series of shifts in scale, from huge to tiny and back again. The first of these is the shift from the macrocosmic scale of Earth Art to the microcosmic scale of Body Art. The preparation for this shift can be seen in three final earthworks. In *Reverse Processing*, 1970, Oppenheim entered guerilla-like at night into barges in the East River that carried unrefined cement from a cement factory, and inscribed huge, white, cancelling X's in each barge in refined cement powder. As with *Cancelled Crop*, what he had in mind was a comment on the artwork. Symbolically returning the processed stuff to its origin, to its preprocessed and prerefined state, implies stopping the artist's pigment from becoming illusion on a canvas, stopping the sculptor's cement from becoming rigid, cancelling the tendency of a style or line of work to become as enduring as bronze; it presages a change, in other words. In a related piece, powdered calcium was returned to the mine whence it had once been removed in unrefined lumps. Carl Andre's gesture of exhibiting unaltered bricks rather than a structure built of them, is related, as is Duchamp's remark that a painting could be reduced to just a canvas and tubes of paint.

Earth Art, the aspect of Oppenheim's work which was now receding, and Body Art, the aspect which was emerging, crossed paths in *Maze*, 1970, a work which was sited in the earth but acted out in the body. (This had already been hinted in *One Hour Run*.) In a field where cattle browsed, an enlarged version of a rat's laboratory maze was installed in the form of walls made of stacked bales of hay. The cows's food was put at the other side of the maze. The cows were led into the maze. As a piece that intended to concretize cognitive processes or to make sculpture of them, the idea was that the cows would be led through the maze daily and after a few days they would have learned their way through it, like big rats. This rearrangement of the cognitive equipment of other beings was to constitute the artwork; the artwork, in other words, existed in the mind of the cattle, was installed in their consciousness. (But the reality of the body overcame the cognitive aspect. When the cows learned where the food was they just ran right for it, knocking down the hay walls.)

Much of what is called Body Art is really an art of rearranging cognitive patterns, that is, of accessing the cognitive realm through the channel of the body. The epistemological aspect of Oppenheim's work was coming to the foreground in the shift from the earth as site to the body as site. (In this sense Oppenheim's work has more in common with Vito Acconci's than with Smithson's, Heizer's, and De Maria's, with their continuing emphases on land masses that suggest pre-Modern ritual zones and states of religious awe.) *Color Application for Chandra*, 1971 (p. 76-77), shows Oppenheim's work developing its coherent theoretical web. To the idea of consciousness as the sculptural material (or really to the idea of cognition, since it is not raw consciousness that has interested Oppenheim, but consciousness as it processes specific materials) Oppenheim conjoined a tendency more or less unique to his oeuvre, to regard his children as composing with him a larger genetic body eligible as a carrier of Body Art. In *Color Application* Oppenheim taught his two-and-a-half-year-old daughter Chandra the names of colors by projecting them and repeating their names; an audio loop of Chandra's voice repeating the color names was played twenty-four hours a day to a parrot until he had learned to say them too, but without the association with the colors. Here a kind of stripping away occurs in which the cognitive signs, the words, are passed on, but without comprehension of their signifieds. Culture has translated into nature, but a lot has been lost in the translation. A kind of transgressive tendency in regard to the limits of the self also appears here. As in *Maze*, the artwork takes place within the minds of other beings; the artist intervenes directly in their cognitive processes without their requesting it.

Various other works from the end of 1970 and the beginning of 1971 advanced the transition into Body Art, introducing both the artist's body and the theme of the endangerment of the body as parameters in relation to real sites in the earth. In *Two Jumps for Dead Dog Creek*, 1970, the artist jumped across the actual creek twice, fusing his body with the dimensions of the natural site. He then repeated the jump from memory on a sand floor in a gallery, embodying the dimensions of the creek in the footprints in the sand. Here the artist's body became the mediating device that brought outside and inside together. As in Smithson's *Non-sites*, an element from nature was brought into the gallery, but not in simple physical fact, as Smithson had it, so much as suspended in the material of cognition and carried in within the artist's body as part, now, of himself.

The scale shift that was involved in the transition from earthwork to bodywork accelerated in *Glassed Hand, Leafed Hand* (p. 56), and *Rocked Hand*, all 1970. In each of these works the right hand progressively covered the left hand with the indicated natural materials. The process was photodocumented. As in *Reverse Processing*, there is a suggestion that culture should return to nature, not in a sentimental quest for salvation by natural forces, but

(continued on page 27)

Overleaf left: Directional Cuts, (detail) 1968. Hamburg, Pennsylvania. Snow fencing. 4' × 100'.
   A linear placement of snow fencing pinpoints true north.

Right: Contour Lines Scribed in Swamp Grass, 1968. New Haven, Connecticut. Swamp grass, aluminum filings. 150' × 200'.
   Contour lines from neighboring mountains are enlarged and plotted on the site with aluminum filings. Because the site is below sea level, the completed project is regularly under water, according to the tides.

Annual Rings, 1968. United States/Canada
boundary at Fort Kent, Maine and Clair, New
Brunswick. Time: U.S.A. 1:30 P.M., Canada
2:30 P.M. Ax, shovel, ice, snow. 150′ × 200′.
   The schema of lines depicting the annual
growth of a tree is mapped as pathways shov-
eled out of snow, and is bisected by the river
that forms the United States and Canadian
boundary line. A collage of scales and a contrast of durable and transient materials (wood
and snow) are used to intertwine and root
together familiar concepts of tree rings,
time zones, and geopolitical boundaries.

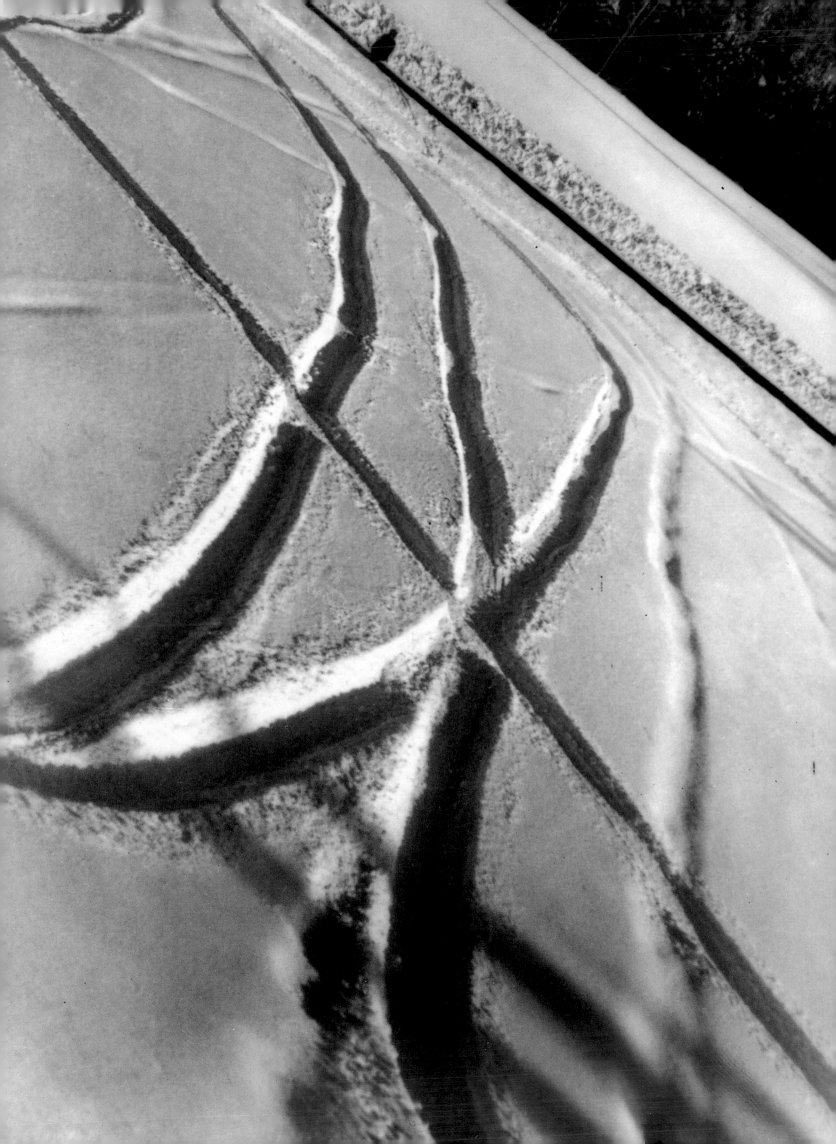

in a relinquishing of the boundaries of the self. The steadily progressing scale shift went to the limit in *Material Interchange*, 1970 (p. 60). In the first stage the artist's semi-detached fingernail was "installed" in a crack in the floor; in the second, a splinter from the floor was installed in the skin of the artist's finger. The transition from *Cancelled Crop* to *Material Interchange* is a massive, multifaceted shift in focus, like turning the cognitive process inside out, from macrocosm to microcosm, outside to inside, object to subject. First the landscape of the artist's body, then that of the mind, has replaced the earth as the privileged site for art.

The Body The use of the body as site brings with it implications of sacrificial rites somewhat paralleling the implications of ancient ritual zones in Earth Art. Both genres had relationships with pre-Modern ideas of the body, the earth, and a sacrificial symbiosis between them. *Cancelled Crop*, for example, could be read in terms of the myth-cluster of the Dying Year God in ancient agricultural societies, a type of seasonal ritual intended to offset the harvesting of the crop by offering a variety of stategies ranging from human sacrifice to withholding a portion of the crop from use. Oppenheim has mostly attempted to distance his work from this level of meaning. In contrast, some artists of his generation who were engaged in related work were explicit about its mythic roots or parallels. In the work of the American artist Carolee Schneeman, for example, and of Viennese Actionists such as Hermann Nitsch, these mythic roots were acknowledged. In the sixties Schneeman revived a neolithic type of orgiastic rite in the realm of Performance Art; Nitsch performed symbolic human sacrifices in his *Orgy Mystery Theater*. Oppenheim entered this area of ritualistic meaning with a pronounced skepticism. The loss of a fingernail, for example, in *Material Interchange* was an ironic gesture toward self-sacrifice, a tiny motion toward a huge surrounding firmament.

This type of understated gesture repeats and entrenches itself in *Reading Position for Second Degree Burn*, 1970 (p. 62), in which Oppenheim lay in the sun for five hours bare-chested except for an open book lying on him. There is a humorous interplay between the ideas of leisure and sunbathing on the one hand, and self-endangerment and sacrifice on the

other. In addition the piece carries for Oppenheim, as always, a comment on the artwork and its possible permutations. "The piece has its roots in a notion of color change," he has said, "I allowed myself to be painted, my skin became pigment."[4]

A series of works in which Oppenheim performed minute physical acts in awkward positions in the gallery setting presaged performative modes of narcissistic bodily presence shared by Joseph Beuys, Dan Graham, and others. In *Extended Armor*, 1970 (pp. 54-55), for example, Oppenheim lay belly-down on the floor with his face wedged into one end of a structure of three boards with a channel in the middle.[5] From the other end of the channel a video camera recorded his face in close-up. Meanwhile, a tarantula was released in the other end of the wooden channel and moved toward him. He fended off the

Gasoline-powered chain saws are used to cut ice at the site of *Boundary Split* in 1968, on the St. Johns River at the United States/ Canada border.

Opposite page: One Hour Run, 1968. St. Francis, Maine. 10-horsepower snowmobile. 1′ × 3′ × 6 miles. Duration: 1 hour.
   A snowmobile, driven continuously for one hour, cuts tracks into the snow.

27

spider's threat by pulling out strands of his own hair, spinning them into balls, and blowing them down the channel with his breath to interrrupt the spider's advance.[6] Like the spider spinning a web, he used his own bodily threads to survive. There is something shamanistic here as he becomes like the spider, adopting its mode of behavior in order to deal with it, but at the same time there is a rejection of heroic poses or a mock heroism.

The complementary themes of self-endangerment-as-art and of gallery critique mingled in *Protection*, 1971 (p. 63-64). An area of land was marked off and protected from incursion by human bodies as if it were a sacred or hellish place; whether the space was being protected from the humans or the humans from the space was debatable. Twelve trained German shepherd attack dogs were tethered to stakes around a rectangle of ground near, but outside of, the Museum of Fine Arts in Boston. The dogs, if they were all lunging at the ends of their tethers, could not quite manage to bite a person walking in and out of the protected space with an exact knowledge of the dimensions involved. (During the realized piece, the dogs mostly slept.) The elaborate security system was in place to protect an inner space that held nothing, that had no reason to be protected, in parody of the nearby museum, with its elaborate protection system for artworks. It was a condemnation of the museum as a place dedicated to an incorrect view of art as an eternal commodity to be sheltered from change and incursion.

Danger   The endangerment of the body, which was a central theme of Body Art, occurred as an artistic theme at about the same time in America in the works of Oppenheim, Acconci, and a few others, in Europe in the works of Klein (especially the *Leap Into the Void*, which was executed in 1960) and the Viennese Actionists, and in Japan in the works of members of the Gutai Group. The tendency arose from widely-felt ideological roots in the anti-Modernist debate, which was a debate of sufficient philosophical consistency that its meanings could be read similarly in unconnected cognitive acts in Europe, America, and Asia. This ideological rift had to do with a contradiction within high Modernism, an era approximately contemporaneous with the Romantic era.

In the Kantian-Hegelian Romantic ideology that underlay the theory of art of Greenberg and his disciples, the artist was believed to act out a heroic role as a metaphysical adventurer going out on the razor's edge of spiritual discovery for the sake of all mankind, whose salvation was conceived as in some way dependent on these gestures as once it had depended on the gestures of renunciate monks. Yet, contrariwise, in actual practice the activity of the artist or poet was completely, even absurdly, removed from any danger to the artist's physical self. The Romantic feeling was that the artist and poet exposed their spiritual selves to a greater danger through their incorporation of the horrific vastness of the sublime as described by Edmund Burke. But in actual physical fact, the artist merely daubed colors with a little brush and the poet merely made marks on paper with a pencil.

The absurd discrepancy and separation between the ideas of spiritual and physical risk was one of the secret inner paradoxes of Modernism that the artists of the critical anti-Modernist period set about exposing and critiquing as if it were a kind of fraud. The insistence of Body artists on putting their actual bodies in danger was a kind of tough guy one-upmanship of the Formalists. Klein jumped off a high ledge without a cushion. Chris Burden, in 1971, had himself shot in the arm as an artwork. Oppenheim's most extreme gesture of this kind was *Rocked Circle—Fear*, 1971 (p. 68), in which he stood in a five-foot-diameter circle for half an hour while a collaborator on the third floor of an adjacent building dropped rocks into the circle. There were no direct hits, but they were close enough to inspire fear; a video camera captured his changing facial expression under the impact of the surges and ebbs of feeling. What is interesting and characteristic about this work is not the macho display—an element more prominent in the Klein and Burden pieces—but the complexity with which cognitive, performative, representational, and theatrical elements intersect in what seems superficially to be a primally simple event. In so far as the fear *is* the artwork, Oppenheim has exhibited an intervention in his own mental processes, echoing *Two Jumps for Dead Dog Creek* and other works.

The Spirit   Oppenheim's work up to this point in his life had carried a heavy burden of theory. It was a

Pages 29-31: Salt Flat, 1968. New York City. Baker's salt. 50′ × 100′.
  One thousand pounds of baker's salt are spread in a rectangle on an asphalt-covered parking lot. Two additional formations of identical dimensions are proposed: one made of one foot by one foot lick blocks to be laid on the ocean floor off the Bahama Coast; the second to be excavated to a depth of one foot in the Salt Lake Desert, Utah.

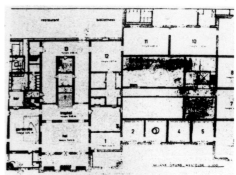

Gallery Transplant, 1969. Jersey City,
New Jersey. 70′ × 70′.

 The literal floor specifications of a gallery
from Amsterdam's Stedelijk Museum are
mapped out on a dirt field in Jersey City. The
photograph of the actual work *in situ* is
shown with two cartographic systems; a map
of Jersey City and a floor plan of the Stedelijk
Gallery.

Removal Transplant—New York Stock Exchange, 1968. 4 tons of paper data. 50′ × 100′ roof area.

"Four tons of paper data from the floor of the New York Stock Exchange are removed, and this residue is transplanted to Park Avenue South, where it is housed in an area defined by the specifications of a roof perimeter. The spatial limits of the exchange floor dictate the manner in which the paper residue organizes itself. In the same way, a cyclone fence directs the accumulation of wind-blown matter, thus functioning as an aesthetic block.

The paper becomes free-moving architectural fuel, undirected, yet responding to the imposition of pre-existing boundaries. The exchange floor is an architectural mold for symbols representing distant locations. Transactions involving a span of three thousand miles take place on the stock exchange floor. The residue [the paper data] at the end of the day carries vestiges of the distance between two points; the point at which a buy order, and the point at which a sell order, is issued. Though it lies dormant on the floor, it is conceptually active. A spatial transaction is implicitly contained in the material; a web of components interact within a continental grid.

At 2:00 P.M. the clearing house floor is filled with the highs and lows of stock transactions—the permutations a stock has undergone during a four hour period. By removing this data from a ground level and carrying it up sixteen stories, I am raising the level of the residue that was actively housed on a lower plane. The material will be held at the top of a building; the building forms a base for the piece. The roof is viewed as a terminal strata for passive information. The Manhattan skyline becomes a tight complex of core samplings of varying depths." (D.O.)

94-95), a tableaux in which a puppet figure, whose face looks like Oppenheim's but whose body is seated like that of a Buddhist monk in meditation, periodically leans forward, striking its head against the rim of a hanging bell. As in *Untitled Performance*, the piece consists in the production of a sound by a body, but now an inorganic body has been substituted for the dog corpse, which, in turn, was a substitute for a living body. The puppet represented Oppenheim's attempted withdrawal from the use of his own body—individual or genetically extended— as an endangered art material. In *Theme for a Major Hit*, 1974 (p. 96), a twenty-four-inch-high puppet was attached to wires that were operated by a machine overhead, causing strange contorted motions to be repeated over and over. The Oppenheim face on the puppet suggests that the artist, despite the Romantic-Modernist myth of his autonomy, is at every moment being manipulated by external forces in ways that do not necessarily make any desirable sense.

Lecture #1, 1976 (pp. 98-99), was also a transition marker. An Oppenheim-faced puppet with lip synch delivered, in Oppenheim's voice, a lecture written by him to an audience of empty chairs, except for one in the back row on which a marionette of a black man was seated, apparently listening. The amusing text announced the marionette's discovery of a conspiracy to murder all the avant-garde artists of Oppenheim's generation, beginning with the death of Smithson in 1973, which was declared a fake accident. The era of Earth and Body Art, the piece seemed to proclaim, was over. The art of pure theory was at an end, and the counterforce was already threatening to destroy it (New Image and the Return of Painting).

In keeping with the end of the age of theory, the piece marks a turn toward representation rather than presence. Earlier works involved living cognition as a material of the piece; here the cognitive process was externally represented—carried out as a communication between puppets. The cognitive thrust now occurs between the artist and the viewer rather than between the artist and his material. The piece initiates a major redirection of Oppenheim's oeuvre into external modelling of the cognitive processes that the earlier work had directly worked with.

The Machines *Beyond the Tunnel of Hate. A Nightmare in Search of Structure.* was installed at Kent State University in 1979. A skeet-throwing machine hurled clay discs down a tunnel into the gallery, where they ricocheted off a trough and met elements called "shape collectors" and "template walls" that directed them to one destination or another. As a site-specific piece, the work incorporated a reference to the shooting of five students at Kent State by the National Guard in 1970. In terms of the anti-Modernist project the piece engaged the gallery

Sterilized Surface, Glass, 1969. Galerie Yvon Lambert, Paris. Commercial glass cleaner, ¼″ plate glass.

Stage 1: application of commercial glass cleaner. Stage 2: removal of cleaner. Stage 3: sterilized surface. The artist applies, then removes cleaner from a plate glass window, producing a surface one-quarter inch away from the gallery interior.

space in a violent confrontation, bringing a real-life danger into a usually sheltered area and cancelling its privileged status as a zone set off from life and the body. Oppenheim characteristically thought of it as a modelling of mental events — a thought speeding unexpectedly into the mind and ricocheting off other mental constructs. As a mechanical representation of thought processes, *Tunnel* bears a noticeable similarity to Duchamp's *Large Glass* (1915-23). Both represent psychology as machinery and apply fantasy names to mechanical parts; Oppenheim's "template walls," for example, recall Duchamp's "Malic Moulds," and so on. The random element created by the different itineraries that the missile could follow, depending upon the variables of path, ricochet, and receptacle, again recall Duchamp—for example, the toy cannon shots that marked unpredictable spots on the *Glass* (the "Nine Shots"). Duchamp's idea was, in part, to drain the Romantic aura out of the artwork both by leaving elements of its design to chance and by rendering it like a mechanical drawing, eliminating the human face and figure in favor of the machine. Oppenheim's works of the next five years or so—the *Factories* or machineworks and the *Fireworks*— would follow this thread far past the limit at which Duchamp left it.

The *Factories* are large, intricate, machine-like sculptures using references to the factory production systems of the past as a way of externally modelling cognitive events. Oppenheim remarked, "machines are a rather perfect device to use as a metaphor for

thinking. [Through these] industrial and mechanical systems . . . I felt I could objectify the mechanics of thought."[9] Mining ore, for example, suggests coming up with an idea. Diamond cutting suggests the refinement of a thought-object. A launching structure suggests the moment of putting a thought into action, and so on.

The *Factories* are part of a long tradition of twentieth century art that sought to avoid the sentimentality of the Romantic idea of the self. They connect—as does much of the art of this age of theory—with the earlier avant-garde age in the years before, during, and after the First World War—the era when Henri Bergson, for example, emphasized the necessity of coming to terms with the machine age and when Filippo Marinetti and the Futurists glorified machines as symbols of liberation. Also in the background lie the machines for making art which Raymond Roussel described in his novel *Impressions d'Afrique* (a theatrical version of which influenced Duchamp in 1911); Duchamp's own *Coffee Grinder*, *Large Glass*, and other works; various fantasy machines devised by the Surrealists;[10] and, from the post-World War II avant-garde era, Jean Tinguely's works, perhaps especially *Homage to New York*, 1960; the Engineering, Art and Technology (EAT) project organized by Billy Kluver in 1968; and the 1969-71 Art and Technology project organized by the Los Angeles County Museum of Art. The machine theme in Oppenheim's work began in 1973 with *Wishing Well* (p. 84) and gradually intensified until it entered the foreground in 1979, about the time of his meeting with Alice Aycock, whose own work was then turning in the direction of large machine-like sculptures.

Something similar was occurring at this time in his close friend Acconci's work also. For both Oppenheim and Acconci the era of directly embodying theory through the use of mental process or consciousness as material had passed, and questions concerning the nature of the physical art object and its representational force had reasserted themselves. In American art history in general something like this was happening. The kenosis, or emptying out, of Minimal and Conceptual Art was replaced by a plerosis, or filling up, in terms of new projects in a reconceived arena, first of sculpture and, very soon, in the works of other artists, of painting.

(continued on page 44)

Block for Future Energy, 1969. Sand, wood, salt blocks. 4′ × 8½′ × 4′.

Trial standing broad jumps are made across Dead Dog Creek in Wisconsin and then onto regular terrain. After the jump is made successfully two times, a single broad jump is repeated on sand in a gallery. A wall is constructed at the midpoint of the sand area after the first jump, to prevent another repeat of the jump.

Ground Mutations, 1969. Kearny, New Jersey and New York City. Duration: 3 months.

Shoes cut with one-quarter-inch diagonal grooves down the sole and heel are worn for three months, leaving behind a pattern of shoe impressions that connect the previous patterns produced by thousands of individuals.

Oppenheim's *Factories* operate on a number of levels of scale. Synaptic and other microprocesses are imaged big and take on a look as of cosmic models, recalling Ezekial's vision in the Old Testament of fiery wheels turning in the sky, or the descriptions of wheels within wheels in Plato's quasi-mechanical conceptions of the universe. Meanwhile, at a middle level of scale, in between the cosmic model and the synaptic exchange, these works suggest the factories and factory machinery they are named after. Some suggest industrial architecture, as architecture stands at times—in the pictures of M.C. Escher, say—as mind stuff objectified. The spaces of the mind, once conceived as a temple, are reconceived as a factory in the spirit of the Industrial Revolution. Others refer, either by their look or by their titles, to types of industrial machinery. *Final Stroke. Project for a Glass Factory.*, 1980 (pp. 130-31), for example, resembles an assembly line or conveyor belt; *The Diamond Cutter's Wedding*, 1979 (pp. 122-23), suggests a quarrying operation; *Impulse Reactor. A Device for Detecting, Entering, and Converting Past Lies Travelling Underground and in the Air.*, 1980 (p. 124), recalls a nuclear reactor; *Launching Structure # 1. (An Armature for Protection). (From the Fireworks Series)* 1981, evokes a missile launcher.

The conflation of industrial and cognitive metaphors in these works is often suggested in their titles. *An Operation for Mining, Elevating, and Converting Underground Memories of a Fifth Season.*, 1980, for example, substitutes the mentalist term "Memories" for a materialist term, such as iron ore or coal, putting the piece into the area of subjectivist or idealist allegory. *Accelerator for Evil Thoughts*, 1982 (p. 144), and *A Device for Detecting, Entering, and Converting Past Lies Travelling Underground and in the Air*, 1980, and others also participate in this deliberate mixing of mental and material references.

The machineworks do not present an idealized or universal model of cognition so much as a series of distinct personalities with different idiosyncracies. "An idea, which arises from the depths of the consciousness," as one critic wrote, "is developed, refined, embellished and transported along a tortuous path. It endures trials and difficulties, highs and lows, and encounters numerous mental blocks in the course of the process."[11] The idiosyncratic differences among Oppenheim's machineworks represent the varying neurotic formations of personalities. Each achieves coherence, as another critic put it, "because of the uniformity and consistency of their madness."[12]

Personalities I will describe the workings of eight of these machines, which the reader can follow by looking closely at the pictures.

1. *Waiting Room for the Midnight Special. (A Thought Collision Factory for Ghost Ships).*, 1979 (p. 119), the piece that led into the machineworks, is a scale model for a large site-specific piece that was never realized. It has four elements: a tunnel that approaches a circular depot or switching device; a "smoke transmission chamber" at about two o'clock on the circle; templates and molds for "ghost ships" farther around the circle; and a V-shaped vent that exits from the circle and goes to the ocean. As in Duchamp's *Notes in the Green Box*, a collection of documents forming a kind of commentary on the *Large Glass*, each element has a name and a description of its function, however fantastical. The switching device waits for something to enter the tunnel, its tracks meanwhile rotating; depending upon the speed of entry, and the speed with which the switching track turns, something coming down the tunnel could shoot directly across the track and exit at once into the central ghost ship; or it could exit at either the smoke chamber or the vent to the ocean. There is, in other words, only one entry point into the system but there are three possible exits, with an uncertainty as to which will eventuate. There is also uncertainty about what these three outcomes represent—the ghost ship implying a transport to the afterlife, the smoke chamber an incineration, and the vent to the ocean an escape from the system into nature. There is even an uncertainty about what the awaited thing is; Oppenheim thinks of it, along the lines of *Beyond the Tunnel of Hate*, as a thought about to enter the mind. In another sense the awaited thing is the sculpture that is never seen, which the machine is

(continued on page 51)

Arm & Wire, 1969. Stills from a 6-minute 16mm black-and-white film made with Bob Fiore.

Shown as a close-up shot, the artist slowly rolls his arm across wire and receives an impression on his skin. There is no distinction made between the material and the tool. What is being made (an impression of the skin) and how it is being made (by impressing the skin on wire) are combined in this action.

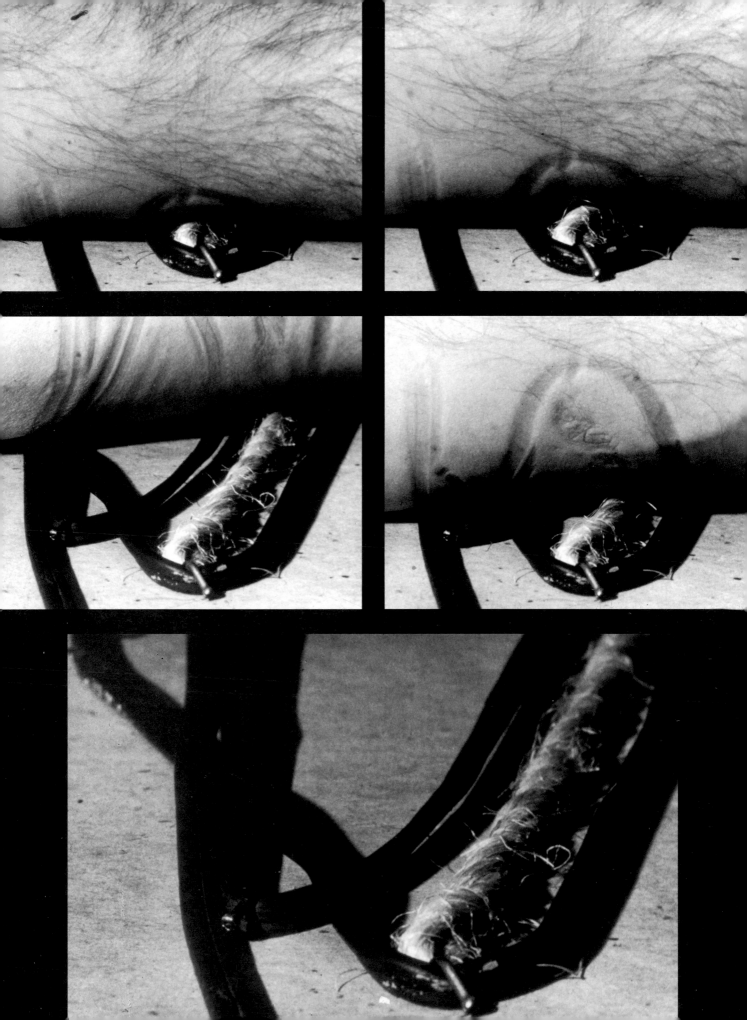

Branded Mountain, 1969. San Pablo, California. Burnt grass. 35′ diameter.

    On a California hillside, a circled X shape is enlarged and burned into the grass. The same configuration that is used to identify cattle now marks a particular place.

Opposite page: Condensed 220-Yard Dash, 1969. Edmonton Art Gallery, Edmonton, Canada. Shoes cut with diagonal grooves down the soles and heels, earth, photography. 5′ × 20′ × 1′.

    While wearing shows with diagonal grooves cut into the soles and heels, a two-hundred-yard dash is made on soft earth. The shoe impressions are cast in plaster, tagged by code, and brought into the gallery, where they are stacked against the wall beneath enlarged stills made from the video of the dash.

Parallel Stress, 1970. Activity. Pier between Brooklyn and Manhattan bridges and an abandoned sump in Long Island, New York. Masonry blocks, earth. Duration of stress position: 10 minutes; position in slump: 1 hour.

The artist tests the capability of his body to suspend itself between two masonry walls. The stress is recorded by the position of his body as it arcs. This arc is then duplicated in an abandoned sump, where the artist assumes the parallel arc position.

only an armature to produce. The work is charming in its simplicity and unclutteredness, almost naive looking, like a child's model railroad. It is difficult to see in it what one author has referred to in Oppenheim's work as its "auto-revelation of its own premises."[13]

2. *Way Station Launching an Obsolete Power. (A Thought Collision Factory in Pursuit of Journey). (A Clip in a Rifle Weapon).*, 1979 (pp. 120-21), is a very different presence. It is blunt and clumsy where *Waiting Room* is transparent and balanced. A cab is being loaded with "ghost bullets" from above—that is the entry; the curved conveyor belt made of metal wheels offers an exit; there is an air-conditioning intake blowing cold air which turns the rotating vents on top of the stacks; a rubber conveyor belt exits on the left, moving continually to the window somewhat like the vent leading out of the system to the ocean in *Waiting Room for the Midnight Special.* The whole massive device is conceived as ready to be launched from a ramp. As in most of the machineworks, only some of the parts really move, because Oppenheim followed Duchamp's immobile fantasy machine rather than the suspect trail of kinetic art with its links to the tradition of aesthetic sculpture.

3. *The Diamond Cutter's Wedding*, 1979 (p. 122-23), represents an early classical stage of this series. Coal or another raw material lies in carts at the left, which are slingshot-mounted in huge rubber straps that, if released, would shoot the carts into the system; these carts are the entry. If released, they pass their materials through the template wall's three differently shaped openings, triangle, square, and arch; this wall acts as a screen or sieve separating the raw stuff by its differently shaped elements. A pendulum behind the template wall swings back and forth, threatening to affect the movement of the particles sifting through. The particles engage the hanging templates on pulleys and are further refined, then move onto three "shape-converters" that have adjustable "photographic blinders" on the other side to adjust the apertures. Finally the stuff falls onto motorized, rotating sieves of the type that are used to separate stones of different sizes. The series of stages in the process represents different transformational characteristics that affect whatever goes through the apparatus.

Sculpturally the work exerts a clear and realized presence. Peering into it one sees a mind that knows where it is going and calmly processes its thought-matter. The diamond that is finally produced is a finished product obtained by a gentle process of refinement that lacks any look of blockage detour, or horror. It is a basically happy view of the unconscious as a machine that produces from mind-stuff the gems of culture. Though there are some variables along the way—such as the question of which shaped doorway the matter passes through in the template wall—and some random or uncontrolled interventions—especially by the swinging pendulum behind that wall—still, the process overall is clear and simple, not like a

Above: Vertical Penetration, 1970. Activity. Aspen, Colorado. Swimming pool, high-diving board. Duration: 15 seconds.
   The specific goal is to pass through air and water from a high altitude.

Opposite page: Preliminary Test for 65' Vertical Penetration, 1970. Activity. Study for a later work. Whitewater, Wisconsin. Gravel mound. Duration: 1 minute.
   Physical condition, output, and performance are extended to their limit, correlated to a particular place and land dimension. In this case, the tolerance factor is sixty-five feet, the height of the Lucky Peak Dam in Wisconsin.

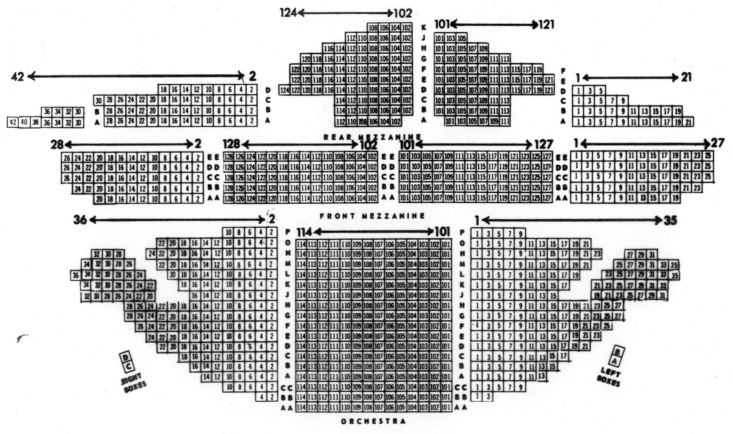

FRONT MEZZANINE ROW "AA" OVERHANGS ORCHESTRA ROW "H"

trap or obstacle course; entry is at one end, exit at the other, and each step along the way represents a progressive refinement with no detours or retrograde movements.

Diamond Cutter shows the *Factories* series having attained its mature power but not yet approaching the point of exhausting its expressiveness and seeking to rejuvenate itself by incorporating new meanings and materials. Consciousness, or thought material, is portrayed from the stage of being a twinge in a synapse in the brain stem to emerging as a fully articulated cultural object, such as an artwork or a philosophy book. The portrayal of the process, from coal lump to diamond, is clear, abstract, and elegantly serene.

4. More threatening is *Saturn Up-Draft*, 1979 (p. 125), which centers around a cage containing a giant juicer or four-bladed cutting device. One entry is via a gasoline-powered sled which could be mounted by a viewer; above it is a vent to exhaust some gaseous residue of unstated, but possibily sinister origin. Another entry is via the raw material sled slingshot-mounted and hovering threateningly in the air. In this piece the mental process begins to cloud over, becoming dangerous and unpredictable. The two divergent entries confuse the beginning of the process, and the center of the process, the whirling cutting device, suggests a violent reduction of the consciousness-stuff, rather than a gentle refining of it. The project is uncertain, though there is an implication that some ethereal byproduct of the material rises through the up-draft cone at the end of the process.

5. In *Caged Vacuum Projectiles*, 1979 (p. 124), the bodies of vacuum cleaners lie on the floor outside a cage; the hoses of the vacuum cleaners enter the cage. The vacuum cleaner bodies out on the floor connect with ovenlike "shape transmission chambers," with three primary-shaped entrance holes. (Again, as in *Diamond Cutter's Wedding*, there is a suggestion of a material universe founded on three elements that, like the elements in Plato's *Timaeus*,

Energy Displacement Approaching Theatricality, 1970. Activity. Whitewater, Wisconsin.

Members of the Art Department of the University of Wisconsin are instructed to swim a fifty-meter freestyle race at maximum energy output. The finish of the race is photographed, and the artists are presented to tickets to the Ambassador Theater, 215 West 49th Street, New York City. Their seating is determined by their placement in the race.

are represented by primary shapes.) It is unclear here exactly where the entry to the process is, what kind of raw material is involved, and what kind of processing it will undergo. The vacuum cleaners give the apparatus a slightly comical air at the same time that they recall Duchamp's snow shovel.

6. In *Crystal Recorder. (Stroking the Throat of Tornado Diane). An Early Warning System.*, 1980 (p. 125), crystal prisms that look like chandelier elements hang from strings that go to pulleys attached to large keys, which look like piano or typewriter keys. In Oppenheim's narrative for the piece, while a writer is typing, the vibration of the keys loosens the chandelier above his head, and eventually the chandelier falls on him; the prisms pierce his head and release the content of what he was writing, which has to do with crystals. So what is happening inside and outside are the same; the macrocosm surrounding the microcosm of consciousness has the same crystalline structure; an elegant solipsistic cosmos is suggested, like jewelled boxes within boxes. The most romantic of the *Factories*, *Crystal Recorder* is a lyrical piece, in stark contrast to the mute, brute presence of *Way Station Launching an Obsolete Power*.

7. *The Assembly Line. (With By-Products from a Mechanical Trance).*, 1980 (pp. 126-27), begins to extend the cognitive modelling into altered states and psychedelic frontiers. There is a metronome at the center of the work, which can't be seen in photographs. An assembly line begins on tables that are suspended from spidery-looking steel structures. The machine is hypnotized and produces a visual correlate of that state in the air sacks that float overhead like dirigibles or balloons. These, the hallucinatory by-products of the machine's trance, float above it like a dream over a dreamer's head. The big bowl that catches the air sack is a kind of cauldron. On the ceiling a revolving wheel-like armature holds the air sacks, potentially placing first one, then another into the cauldron. The hypothetical product of the transformation of the hallucinated air sack in the cauldron is the artwork itself, which is never seen and is not directly under the control of the dreaming, hypnotized, or hysterical artist.

8. In *Occasion for Expansion—A Combat of Structural Projections*, 1981 (p. 132), this psychedelic tendency runs amuck. Two performers, a man and a

(continued on page 58)

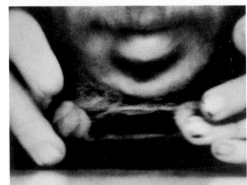

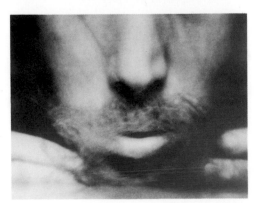

Extended Armor, 1970. Performance. Reese Palley Gallery, New York City. Boards, amplifier, spider, hair, video camera. Duration: 55 minutes.

The artist prevents a tarantula from moving toward his face by ripping out pieces of his hair (*left*) and blowing them through a channel at the oncoming spider (*opposite page*).

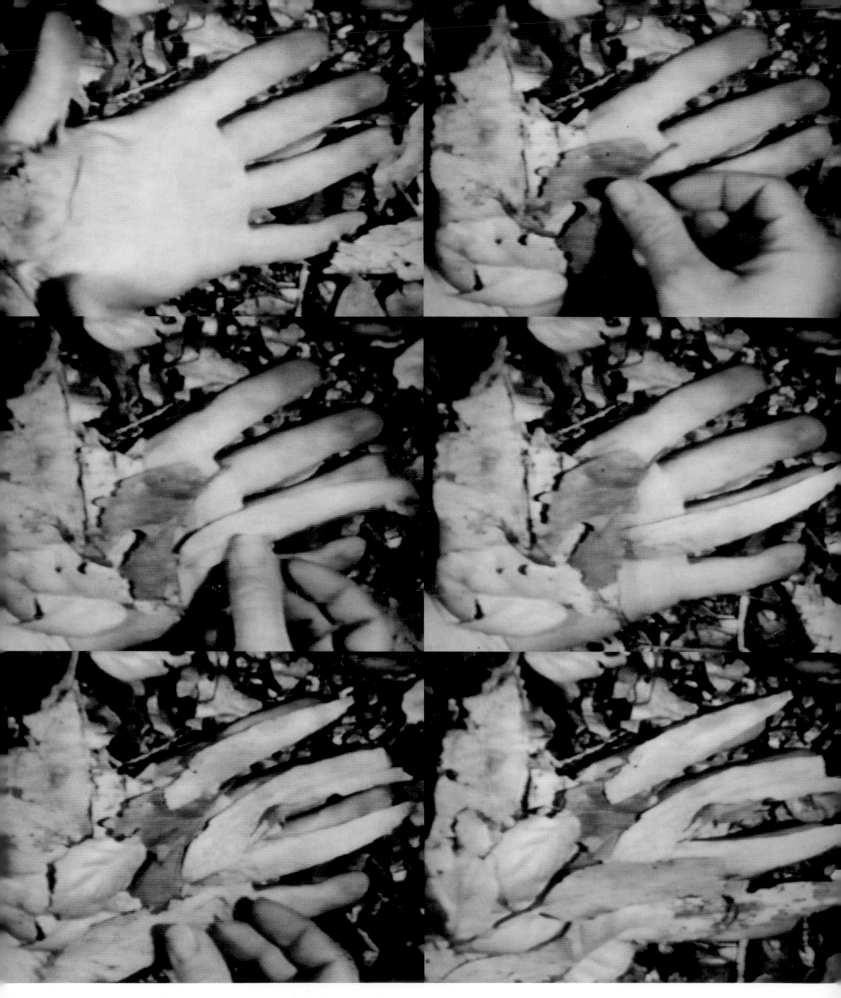

Leafed Hand, 1970. Stills from a 3-minute 16mm color film. Aspen, Colorado. Hand, leaves.

   One hand slowly covers the other with leaves. The right hand renders the left invisible, blending it into the surroundings.

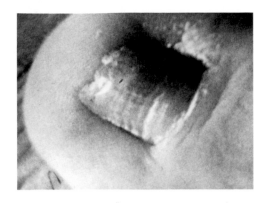

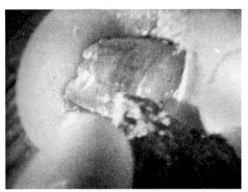

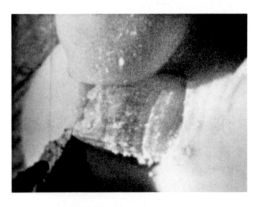

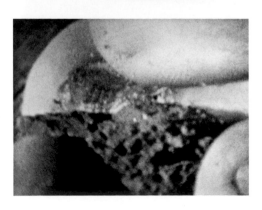

KAISER FOUNDATION HOSPITALS

CHART FACE SHEET

PRIVATE

Nail Sharpening, 1970. Stills from a 6-minute, 8mm black-and-white film.

After dropping a brick on his big toe, the artist engages in the traditional sculptural act of depleting a surface. In sanding his toenail, a ritual of self-reduction, sensations pass from one part of the body to another; he oscillates between being an instigator and a victim. *Above:* the documentation includes a clinical progress report from the Kaiser Foundation Hospital.

woman, lie on hammocks that attach to a huge bellows. Over them hang tanks of exotic gases. These are medical gases which put you to sleep and produce dreams of different types—trylene, for example, which is used as an anaesthetic in abortions and is said to give vivid technological dreams. The performers first breathe the exotic gases, then engage in sexual intercourse, activating the bellows through their undulations. Pressure from the bellows goes through many channels and ends by pumping up the stacks of an expanding industrial city on the left, which represents the hallucination experienced by the lovers; this city expanded by their act of love *is* their chemically induced dream or shared hallucination. The dream city rises from clusters of tubes like a big bagpipe or pipe organ. Hovering in the air over the pipes are suspended discs that could be lowered onto the tops of the stacks, thus shutting them off. The discs are attached, through a system of ropes and pulleys, to rings that control the shape of a giant balloon-airship, giving it the appearance of an atomic explosion when inflated by the ignition of the butane gas tank beneath it. The whole apparatus is controlled by the sex-activated bellows.

This piece, with its organic connection of sex and catastrophe, relationship and disaster, explores terrain far from the simple cognitive transaction of *Waiting Room* or the refined clarity of intuition in *Diamond Cutter's Wedding*. Here, the idea from which the series ostensibly began has gone out of control. It represents a stage when the *Factory* works become increasingly linked to invisible purposes and indefinable processes, with unknown materials undergoing transformations of place and quality whose effect cannot be predicted or described.

Occasion for Expansion is the closest of the *Factories* to the complex sex-based machine-cluster system portrayed in fantastic plan in Duchamp's *Large Glass*. The bellows, for example, recalls Duchamp's bellows-like portrayal of the bride, both in the painting by that title of 1912 and in the *Large Glass*, and the bride's exhalation in the *Glass* of a cloud of sexual feeling. It is also, after two years in which Oppenheim conceived and produced one of these massive works every month or so, about to explode from conceptual overload. Cluttered, unstable, unserene, and unsimple, it is a masterpiece of the series, but a terminal masterpiece, in which the idea behind the

series has intensified itself to the point of spilling over into hysteria. The causal sequence from dream gas to sex act to dream city to mushroom cloud is conceptually unclear though provocative and imbued with a vaguely poetic sense of unspecified yet ominous meaning.

Over a period of about three years the *Factory* works emerged, found their identity, and wandered from it. Losing site of the original motive of modelling cognitive processes as machine-like, they began to take odd, unpredictable turns that have a variety of relationships to human life. Some recall mystical allegories like the fantastical devices of alchemists, but leave the transcendentalist implications unfulfilled; others may be compared to Beuys's systems of batteries and filtration devices, but without their implications of holistic therapies. In terms of history, they suggest both machines of bygone days and an inscrutable technology from another species or another world—machines that don't work in our world or for us, but which seem to suggest another humanity or another reality for which they did once work—or will someday.

The Fire The hysterical overload that characterized *Occasion for Expansion* took over the subsequent development of the series, becoming the basic force of the final mind machines called *Fireworks*. The *Fireworks* consummate what the *Factories* implied. If the late *Factories* show the mind getting ready to shoot off its contents, the *Firework* pieces show it doing so. The *Factories*, to put it differently, "enact the goings-on inside the mental plumbing of creation as a mystery play,"[14] while the *Fireworks* focus on the climactic moment of the mystery—the Transfiguration, so to speak—and enact it over and over. The *Factories* represent displays of thought processes that have cooled down and solidified enough to be looked at. The *Fireworks* show them heating up out of control again. (The artist's earlier works with flares and sky-writing lie in their background.) Again I will describe only a sampling of these large and complex works.

Formula Compound. A Combustion Chamber. An

(continued on page 65)

Stomach X ray, 1970. X rays, color photography. 40″ × 60″.
The traditional method of shaping materials by hand is seen in an X ray of the inside of the artist's stomach as he presses his hands into his rib cage. The stomach is an explanatory surface, releasing sensations of what it "feels like to be formed."

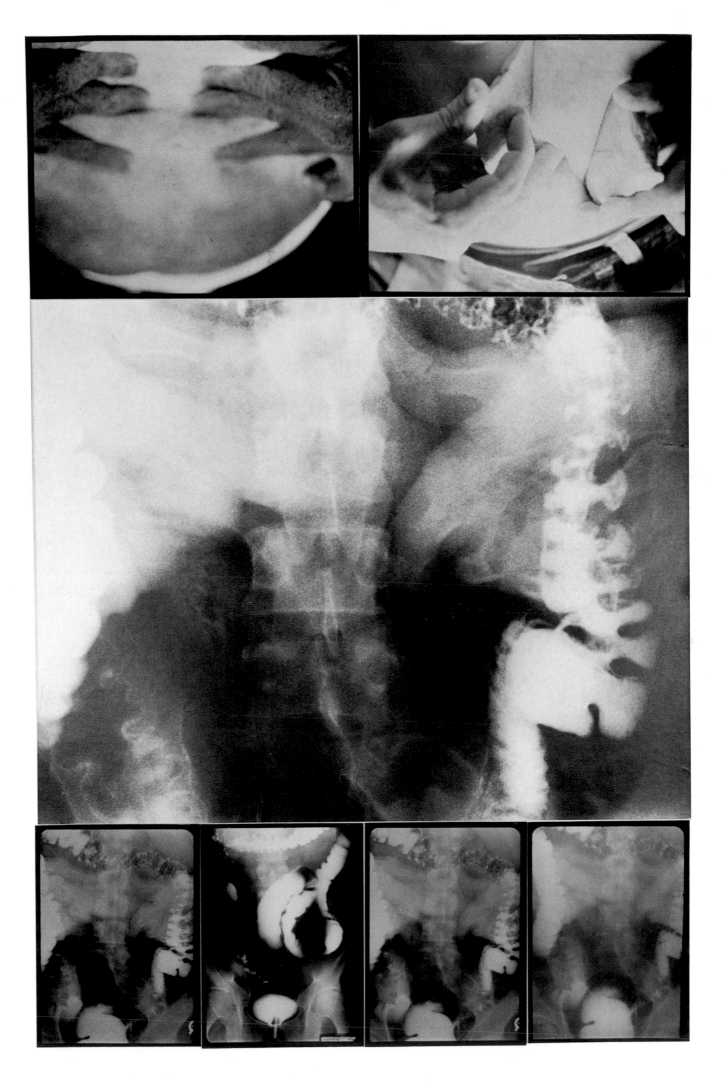

Material Interchange, 1970. Microscope, microprojectors, slides,
fingernail, floorboards. Aspen, Colorado.
  Stage 1: the artist's fingernail is lodged between the gallery floorboards. Stage 2: a splinter from a gallery floorboard is lodged under
the skin of his finger.

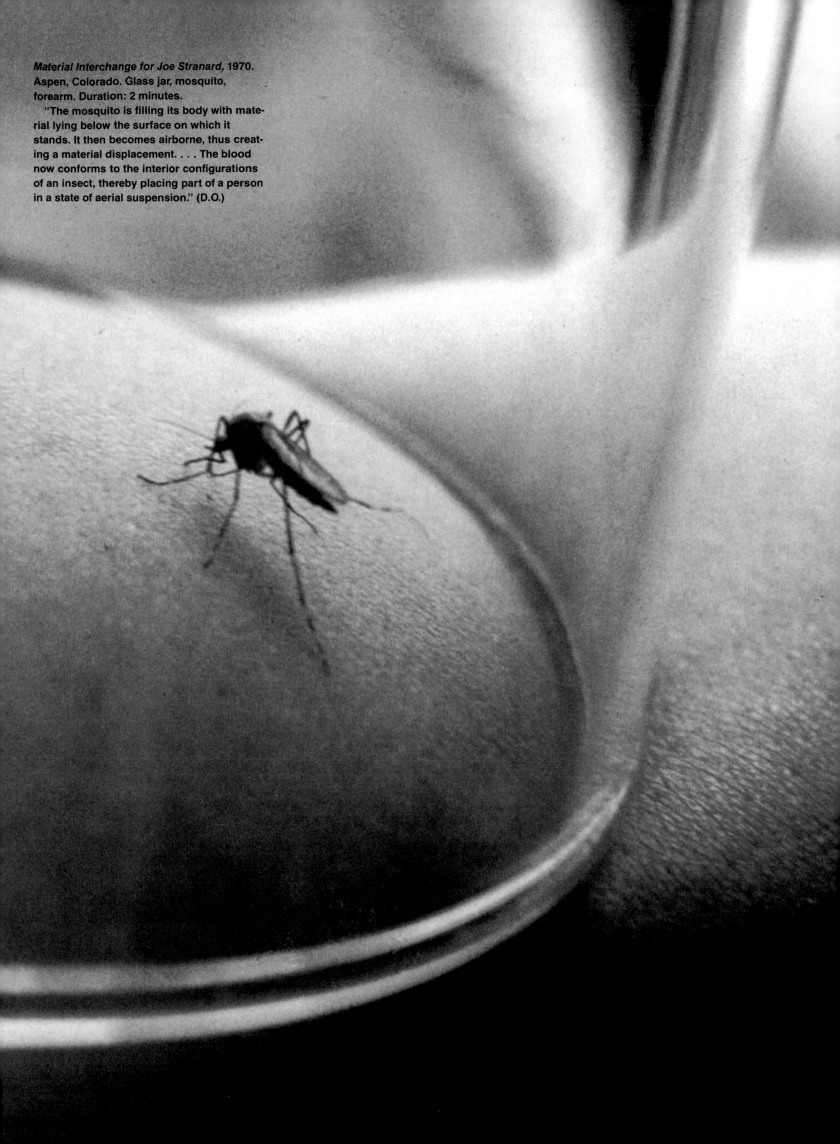

Material Interchange for Joe Stranard, 1970. Aspen, Colorado. Glass jar, mosquito, forearm. Duration: 2 minutes.

"The mosquito is filling its body with material lying below the surface on which it stands. It then becomes airborne, thus creating a material displacement. . . . The blood now conforms to the interior configurations of an insect, thereby placing part of a person in a state of aerial suspension." (D.O.)

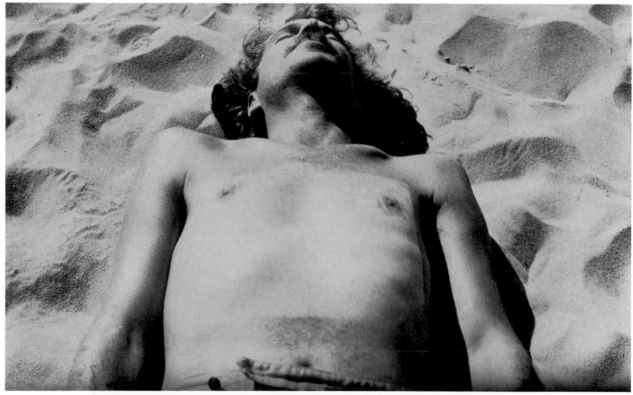

Reading Position for Second Degree Burn, 1970. Jones Beach, New
York. Skin, book, solar energy. Duration of exposure: 5 hours.

"The piece incorporates an inversion or reversal of energy expendi-
ture. The body is placed in the position of recipient . . . an exposed
plane, a captive surface. The piece has its roots in a notion of color
change. Painters have always artificially instigated color activity. I
allow myself to be painted—my skin becomes pigment. I can regulate
its intensity through control of the exposure time. Not only do the skin
tones change, but change registers on a sensory level as well. I feel
the act of becoming red." (D.O.)

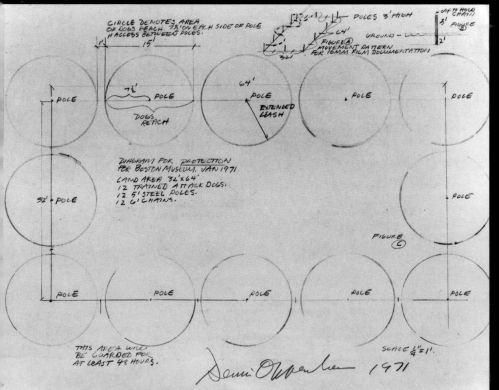

Protection, 1971. Museum of Fine Arts, Boston. 12 trained attack dogs positioned on 32' × 64' land area, 12 5' steel poles, 12 6' chains. Duration: 48 hours.

To exaggerate the preciousness that objects take on by being placed inside an art museum, trained German shepherd dogs *(preceding page* and *above)* are hired to patrol a site adjacent to the Boston Museum. The blue line drawing *(left)* shows where the dogs are stationed. Their movements differ from untrained animals. The question is raised whether an untrained artist can become a part of the museum system.

Exorcism. (From the Fireworks Series)., 1982 (pp. 140-43), was erected on the beach. Looking like an amusement park in miniature, it featured rockets, fountains, and flares mounted on an armature of ladders, suspended bridges, and transparent spinning cylinders. Around it on the sand stood a number of shields with little windows, mounted on upright frames, behind which spectators could stand and be safe from its fiery expressiveness. (Compare the *Viewing Stations*.) Ignited at night in the midst of nature (as Oppenheim had earlier sited large flare works out of doors on Long Island), the work was an orgasmic explosion that did not invite cool and analytic thought from the spectators so much as a nervous combination of silence and laughter.

Launching Structure #2. (An Armature for Projection). (From the Fireworks Series)., 1981-82 (pp. 134-35), had shields with windows mounted on four-wheel bases that could be steered here and there to get different views of the action. Even so, when the ignition came—this time indoors, in a gallery in New York's Soho district, on an evening when only critics had been invited to preview it—the huge complex structure laced everywhere with fireworks created havoc and cleared the gallery. Mobile towers with tanks of butane gas were used to ignite the different areas; wheels turned, chain reactions occurred, fires swept down swooping ramps as from the sky, and the piece exploded like a house of cards. Some viewers hit the floor, others headed for the door. The fire department came and broke the windows to clear the smoke. Everyone's clothing had burn marks from flying sparks. The sparking synapses of hysterical mental processes had become a model for a universe out of control and exploding in a kind of terminal orgasm, both big bang and black hole at once.

Pause There followed a period of latency, quiescence, and reconsideration. After five years, roughly 1979-84, of intense and constant production, Oppenheim devoted a period to reading, thinking, tending to his physical health, and refeeling his place in the world and that of his art. When he dove energetically into a new line of work, significant changes had occurred. His work had, of course, always involved periodic changes of direction, unlike the safer signatured oeuvres of some of his contemporaries.

This change, however, which began to reveal itself in a new series in 1987, was somewhat different in scale. It involved a meta-change in the sense of history—which is to say, of purpose—that supported the motivation of the oeuvre. This change reflected events in the surrounding cultural mood.

The philosopher Arthur Danto proclaimed in his 1984 essay "The End of Art" that, according to his understanding of the Hegelian (which is to say Modernist) view of history, art had reached its culmination in the Conceptual period. Danto was referring to early conceptual pieces that involved working with pure cognition ("Spirit") as much as possible. Having become pure Spirit, in this view, art had worked out its historical imperative and had no further place to go. But for the practitioners themselves, the sense of historical imperative did not seem to pass away with their early work. The Earth Art and Body Art movements were still Modernist in the sense that the artists involved felt they were carrying on, stage by stage, a certain evolutionary unfolding of awareness. For Oppenheim, this feeling extended to the period of machineworks, which still seemed to be somehow intuiting avenues of civilization yet to come—or, at least, gesturing hypothetically toward them. It is true that Oppenheim and some of his peers had rejected painting, but they had not rejected the whole Modernist myth of historical advance with it. On the contrary, their rejection of painting was for the sake of going beyond it, stretching the envelope of art history into new regions, climbing yet higher on the Modernist hierarchy of linear ascendance. Indeed, though the sense of historical inevitability that had characterized high Modernist art began to deteriorate with Pop Art in about 1962, it was not until about 1983 or 1984 that post-Modernism, or post-History, became a pervasive and mainstream attitude in the visual arts. This altered shape of things came through to Oppenheim at that time, in part through his reading of Jean Baudrillard and other post-Structuralist authors, with their intensified focus on the incoherencies and discontinuities of things. The post-Structuralist sense of the disintegration of the Modernist paradigm of reality was a difficult confrontation for Oppenheim and others of his generation who had felt that they were helping to push history over the top by freeing art from archaic aesthetics and rendering it cognitively self-aware.

Coming out of his period of reorientation, Oppenheim found that the motivation of history was no longer as available as it once had been. There was no longer an overriding sense that an evolutionary force inherent in the work was propelling it onwards through the envelope of history. Not only did the nature of his work change with this realization, but his discourse about it developed an exacerbated sense both of humor and of darkness, in place of the pseudo-scientific distance of his earlier utterances. Of course, there had been dangerous and ominous elements in his work from the beginning, but they had been contextualized within the sense of an onrushing history. The black humor already present, for example, in the text of *Lecture #1*, 1971, with its conspiracy of assassinations, was about history, its inner purposes, and the obstacles to them. But now, beginning in about 1987, Oppenheim spoke as if this basic matrix were gone. He referred to a disarray in the world around him, described images as having "jitters," and spoke of his work as "objects in their terminal condition," expressions of "the disease of the real," "symptoms of overload," and so on.[15] The "image jitters" that Oppenheim spoke of in connection with his work of the late 1980s came in part from the sense of no longer being securely embraced by a surrounding matrix of history that assured meaning. It was the jitters of waking up alone in the meaningless landscape of post-Modern or post-Historical culture, where the motive for making art could no longer rise from a meta-narrative.

Jitters At this time Oppenheim began to make smaller works that can be seen as parts broken off from hypothetical larger works and invested with a hyperintensity of individual focus. Cut loose from a sense of history (which is to say, meaning), they stand alone in the surpassingly weird lunarscape that their own strangeness implies. Though it would be an exaggeration to describe Oppenheim at this time as a committed post-Modernist, his works of the late eighties embody the post-Modernist deconstructive force of disintegrationist critical thought more acutely than perhaps any other sculptures of their day. They are beyond the late-Pop pseudo-kitsch of Jeff Koons in their oddness and, occasionally, their analytic contemplation of bad taste. Their humanistic size represents a rejection of Modernist monumental synthesis. They are disconnected fragments of narratives that either have fallen apart or were never really held together except by the projected emotions of wishful thinking. They aver both the reduced ambitions and the permission, or relaxation, of the post-Historical moment.

A unifying theme that occurs in many of these pieces, offsetting the euphoric Modernist sense of immortality underlying the bodyworks and genetic-works, is an exacerbated awareness of mortality. The theme is expressed sometimes through motifs of animal energy, heat, and breath, at other times through motifs of threat, tremor, and amputation. *Steam Forest with Phantom Limbs* (p. 160) and *Stove for High Temperature Expression*, both 1988, involve heating coils installed at the tops of fiberglass tree trunks. On the heating coils stand glass bowls of water, which the heating apparatus will turn to steam. The bowls have faces and serve as replacement heads for the decapitated stumps. The decapitated being represented by the tree trunk is thus offered the opportunity of reappearing in other forms, transferred from solid to liquid to vapor. A primitive idea of spirit as an energy that leaves an overheated body informs both these works and a number of others. In *Hot Voices*, 1989, three-feet-wide masks with flames coming out of their mouths repeat the primitive theme of spirit as breath, as speech, and as a fiery exhalation of an excited—or dying—organism.

The heating coils and tree trunks of those works inject the theme of heat-spirit into the domestic and common stuff of everyday life. (Perhaps in this there is a memory trace of Duchamp's use of domestic implements such as a snow shovel and a bottle rack in his "readymades"). The same theme informs *The Appliance Spirit* series, 1988, which are cookstoves whose heating coils extend upward into spring-like beings, one human and one quadruped, which rise as spirit-forms or attenuated bodies from their emanation of heat. In *Digestion: Gypsum Gypsies*, 1989 (pp. 176-77), the relationship between animal body and heat is reversed; the heat arises as a sign of health and vitality from the bodies of forest animals. Five deer are disposed around a space (one halfway through a wall) with butane flames shooting from their antlers. The piece has a presence of both surprise and recognition, and a quasi-surreal sense of the rightness of wrongness.

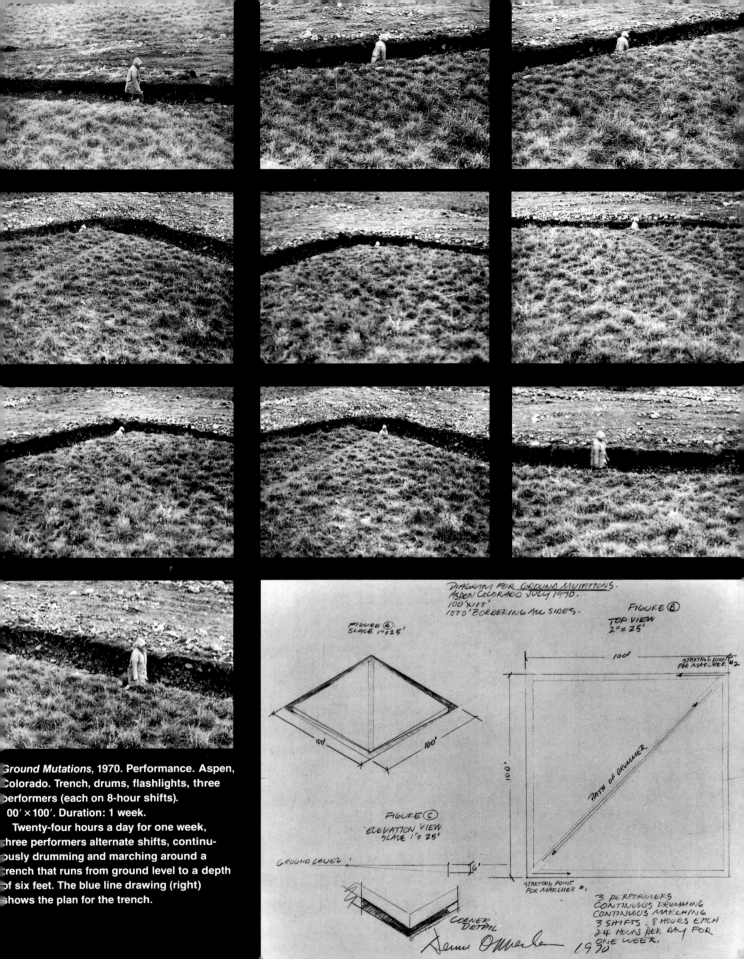

Ground Mutations, 1970. Performance. Aspen, Colorado. Trench, drums, flashlights, three performers (each on 8-hour shifts). 100′ × 100′. Duration: 1 week.

Twenty-four hours a day for one week, three performers alternate shifts, continuously drumming and marching around a trench that runs from ground level to a depth of six feet. The blue line drawing (right) shows the plan for the trench.

DIAGRAM FOR GROUND MUTATIONS.
ASPEN COLORADO JULY 1970.
100'X100'
1000' BORDERING ALL SIDES.

FIGURE Ⓑ
TOP VIEW
2" = 25'

FIGURE Ⓐ.
SCALE 1" = 25'

STARTING POINT
FOR MARCHER #2

100'

PATH OF DRUMMER

STARTING POINT
FOR MARCHER #1

100'

100'

100'

FIGURE Ⓒ
'ELEVATION VIEW'
SCALE 1" = 25'

GROUND LEVEL

6'

CORNER
DETAIL

3 PERFORMERS.
CONTINUOUS DRUMMING
CONTINUOUS MARCHING
3 SHIFTS. 8 HOURS EACH.
24 HOURS PER DAY FOR
ONE WEEK.
1970

Rocked Circle—Fear, 1971. Activity. Brooklyn, New York. Rocks, chalk, video camera, still camera. Duration: 30 minutes.

"A situation is created which allows registration of an exterior stimulus directly through facial expression. As I stand in a five-foot diameter circle, rocks are thrown at me. The circle demarcates the line of fire. A video camera is focused on my face. The face is captive, its expression a direct result of the apprehension of hazard. Here, stimulus is not abstracted from its source. Fear is the emotion which produces a final series of expressions." (D.O.)

The fiery apparition of the deer conveys a hint of an idyllic power in nature that one can also sense, understatedly, in some of the earthworks, but that is just as clearly controverted in other works where nature is presented as a kind of dysfunction. In *Above the Wall of Electrocution*, 1989 (p. 165), animal masks are attached to inflatable fabric bodies that have been turned inside out, pulled out through the mouths of the masks, and hung from a rack overhead with devices to inflate and deflate them periodically. One of Oppenheim's most discomfiting pieces, *Above the Wall,* suggests a slaughterhouse or a selfhood gone berserk and imploded.

Other works express not just the primitive cult of animal energy, but an anxiety about losing it in a tremor, misfire, or implosion. These works often convey an intense bodily uneasiness that is presented with a Beckett-like matter-of-factness or coolness. In *Thought Bones from Between the Fingers of Fear*, 1988, fiberglass casts of human thigh bones with blades inserted into their ends are driven into the gallery wall or into a timber on the floor. In *Tremor*, 1988, human teeth chatter under a hot light on top of a pole. *Virus*, 1988 (p. 171), and *Bad Cells Are Comin'*, 1989, radiate a fear of cellular disorder that, in reference to art, is conflated with the spread of kitsch. In *Virus*, a lattice-like armature is punctuated with Mickey Mouse effigies. *Bad Cells Are Comin'* is a ring of drum-set cymbals with sac-like laboratory bottles of black ink attached, a butane torch rotating in the center heating all the bottles, and no one present. While the grotesque and the tragic mingle in these works, there is also a wry dose of gallows humor in them.

Black Pool, 1990 (p. 170), involves a pool table covered with black felt, with stacks of bowling balls for legs, and above it a kind of genetic model made of black pool balls. In Oppenheim's mind it expresses "genetics gone amuck."[16] A gene, like a pool ball, misses its destination and ricochets around the available arena; the pattern of its misplaced movement is three-dimensionalized in the lattice structure above the table. The title, *Black Pool*, punning on pool table, refers to a gene pool as a game, and suggests the operations of nature are most perfectly realized in errors and random developments that rewrite the rules. "There's something natural about how things fall apart," Oppenheim remarks.[17] (One has here at least to recall Duchamp's idea that chance, which is in a sense error, reveals a purer or more universal purpose than design.)

In 1989 the *Power Tool* series (p. 166) began, works which include tools that made them as parts of the piece's "auto-revelation of its own premises." In *Four Spinning Dancers*, 1989 (p. 166), for example, the dancers' bodies, made of accumulations of different-sized buffing disks, are mounted on the upright shafts of electrical drills that would ordinarily hold those disks singly and that now hold a whole construction of them and spin them around. As they spin, they appear to have skirts flying in the air. Similarly in *Vibrating Dolls*, 1989, a group of electric saws shakes the dolls up and down in a motion referring to sexual intercourse. Oppenheim's use of dolls harks back to the use of marionettes a decade earlier.

Murder in Hawaiian Shirts, 1990 (p. 161), shows the fish and squid represented on two garishly printed short-sleeved summer shirts becoming three-dimensional and crawling toward one another. The piece suggests poisonous feelings or impulses coming out of human beings and moving toward other human beings. As a comment on art or culture, it expresses a dread of kitsch imagery, which here is becoming an external force through human adoption of it.

Slow Clap for Satie, 1989 (p. 173), shows two trees mounted on revolving pedestals, with large transparent masks of human heads hanging upside down from the branches, flanking a piano-shaped table that appears to be clapping with huge wooden hands. It is a surprising object that one had not expected to see. On the other hand, it is recognizably Oppenheim's work. It shows, for example, his method of collapsing different stages of a process into one object—the piano doing the clapping is rather like the tools being the work. What is unusual in terms of Oppenheim's oeuvre is that it involves an homage to another artist who is named, and specifically to an artist associated with the primal avant-garde period early in this century.

This turn toward homage and art historical reference recurs in *Kissing Racks*, 1990 (p. 181), which incorporates enlarged replicas of Duchamp's *Bottle Rack*. This rare "quotational" moment in Oppenheim's art is especially significant. It represents not

(continued on page 74)

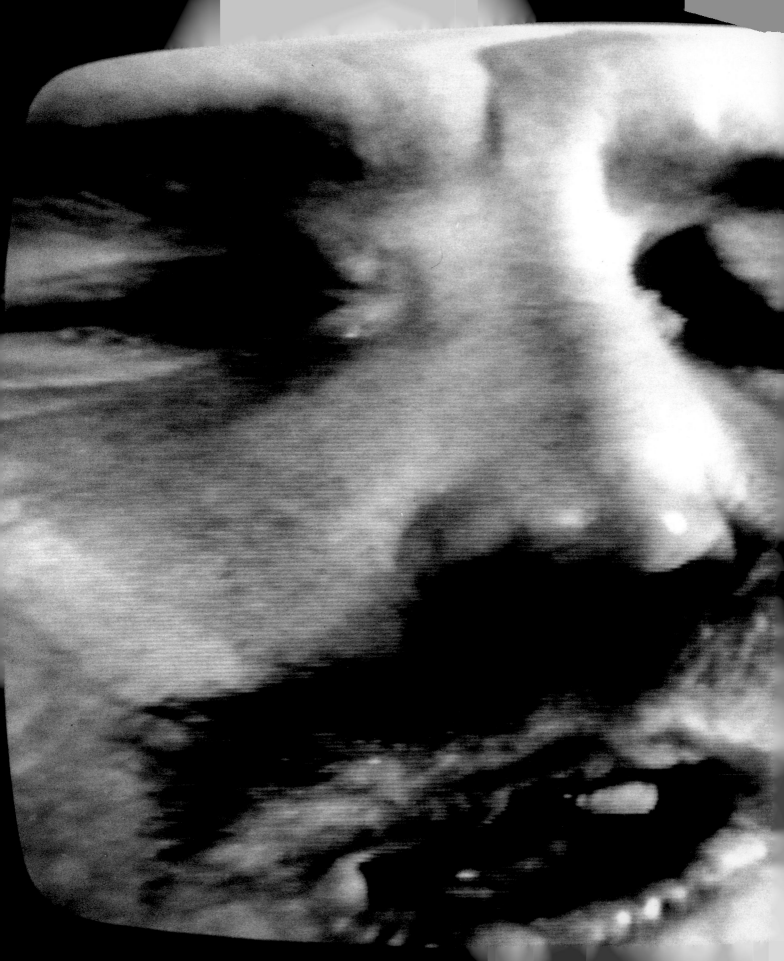

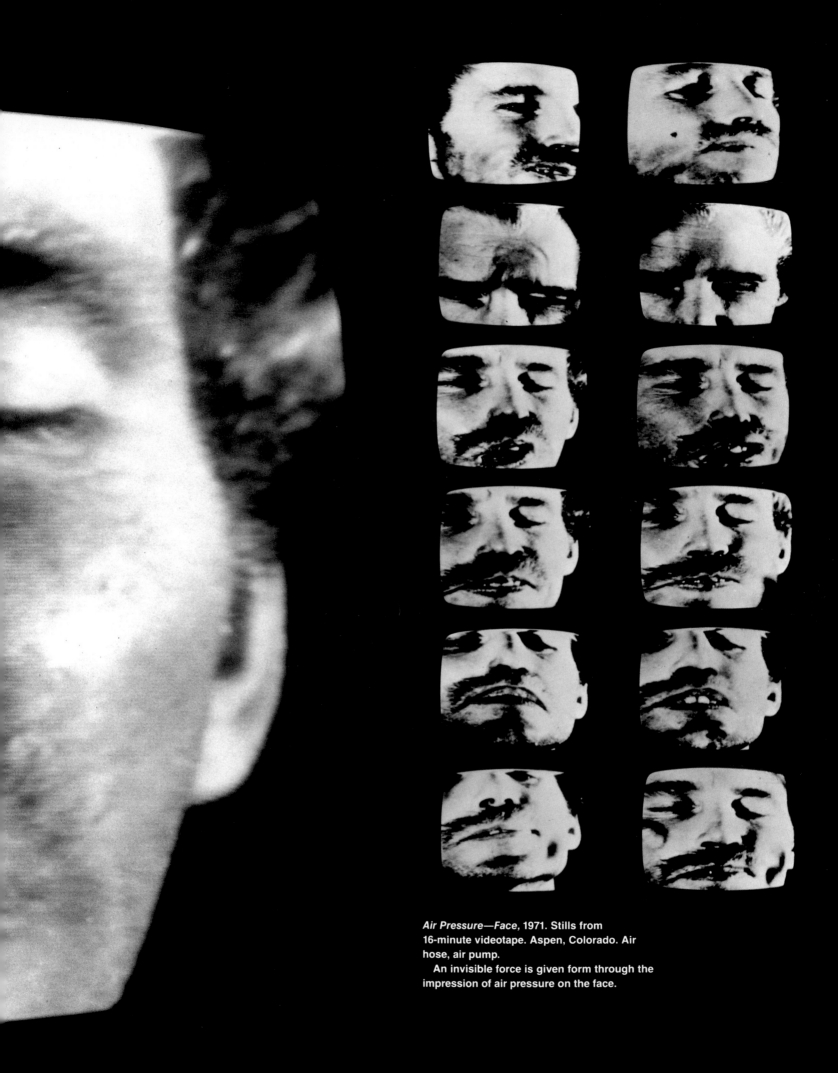

Air Pressure—Face, 1971. Stills from
16-minute videotape. Aspen, Colorado. Air
hose, air pump.
   An invisible force is given form through the
impression of air pressure on the face.

Two-Stage Transfer Drawing. (Returning to a Past State). Dennis to Erik Oppenheim. 1971. *Insert: Two-Stage Transfer Drawing. (Advancing to a Future State). Erik to Dennis Oppenheim.* 1971. Boise, Idaho. Felt-tip markers, wall, human backs.

"As I run a marker along Erik's back, he attempts to duplicate my movement on the wall. My activity stimulates a kinetic response from his memory system. I am . . . drawing through him. Because Erik is my offspring, and we share similar biological ingredients, his back . . . can be seen as an immature version of my own. . . . In a sense, I make contact with a past state." (D.O.) When the roles are reversed *(insert),* and Erik draws on his father's mature back, he makes contact, in a sense, with his future state.

only his acknowledgement of a sense of artistic root-edness in the opening up of options that Duchamp is perceived as historically initiating, but also his acceptance of the post-Modern moment as one condition of his present work.

Development   Like Klein, Duchamp, and a handful of others in the experimental anti-Modernist mode, Oppenheim has tossed off works on which another artist might have constructed a whole career. The diversity and changeableness of his oeuvre have seemed to some to indicate an instability of purpose or lack of overall coherence. One critic questioned, for example, whether his oeuvre showed "development." "There is change in his career," he noted, "but not 'development.' "[18] The question is not simple. To begin with, there are exceptionally clear and strong developmental sequences within large areas of the work. The Land Art period, the Body Art period, the marionette works, and the *Factories* and the *Fireworks*—each of these sequences separately exhibits a strong and clear internal development. It might be asked then, whether there is a sense of development that bridges the gaps and encompasses all these phases. Various opinions could be offered on that point, but a more relevant question may be whether, or how, it matters.

Lead Sink for Sebastian, 1970. Performance. San Francisco. Performer, lead pipe, butane torch, rope, video camera. Duration: 30 minutes.
  The performer is an amputee. A hollow lead pipe is substituted for his wooden leg. A portable butane torch is strapped to his left leg and lit. As the torch melts the lead, his body sinks.

The idea that one developmental sequence has to be traceable through an entire oeuvre may be an outdated Modernist anxiety, deriving as it does from the sub-Hegelian teaching of Karl Schnaase in 1831, from an age obsessed with the idea that History is the temporal embodiment of Reason. This was the tradition behind Greenberg's approach, with its preoccupation with formal development. Oppenheim's work, with its emphasis on discontinuities and ruptures, implies a different, more dialectical, relationship to the sense of evolution. In fact, a kind of *Aufhebung*, or overleaping of the self through incorporation of its other, underlies a lot of the shifts in Oppenheim's sequences. In this, the work seems to offer an analogue to the art history of a changing and volatile era—an era when the Hegelian idea of Spirit as the moving force of art became mobile, the Spirit moving restlessly from one lode to another for its fuel. It is arguable that Oppenheim's shifts have not been strictly in response to this generalized shifting of the Spirit of things, but that, in part, they have been a guiding force of the series of shifts.

America experienced late Modernism in a peculiarly puritanical way that involved a series of discrete "isms", each of which was emphatic in its insistence on purity. The European case was very different. While America was bridging the gap between Modernism and post-Modernism with a series of post-Greenbergian puristic encampments on history—Color Field painting, Minimal sculpture, Primary Shapes, Conceptual Art, Earth Art, Body Art, Site-specificity, Pop Art, Camp, New Image painting, Bad painting, Pluralism, Neo-Expressionism, Quotationalism, Simulationism, Neo-Conceptualism—Europe was in a more amorphously shifting age of synthesis. The post-war period in Europe can be characterized through reference to a type of Leonardian multi-media career exemplified by a few iconic figures, for example, Klein, who practiced painting, sculpture, performance, Conceptual Art, Minimal Art, and, in an odd sense not previously discussed, Simulationism. The outlines of Klein's career are similar in their catholicism to the record of Beuys's oeuvre, Jannis Kounellis's, and other artists's. I don't mean to invite specific comparisons between the works of these European figures and Oppenheim's, or attempts to elucidate one oeuvre by appeals to the discourses about the other. I just mean

to point at a species of artistic career since the Second World War that has felt free to enter any area, engage any genre or material, and continually rearticulate itself in escalating but always rigorous intellectual terms. Oppenheim's oeuvre seems to have embodied both approaches. While going with the appropriate shame and guilt through the puritanical stages of the American sequence, he has at the same time demonstrated the European, all-engulfing, post-Hegelian, omnivorous promiscuity of a History that includes many histories.

The oeuvre as a whole (and it is not complete) has both an air of deathly awareness and an insouciant joyousness of action. I will conclude my discussion by comparing Oppenheim's oeuvre to two of its constituent works that might be used as emblems of it.

Object with a Memory, 1983 (p. 147), was a large, houselike construction that was conceived as a camera or cameralike reality-processing device. As it takes a picture, it contorts and an image comes out of it into physical reality. Each picture the construction takes becomes a part of it, as memory but also physically. In fact, part of its structure is the tools with which it was made—from the pencils with which it was initially sketched out to the saws with which its wooden parts were cut. It is constituted, in other words, by its memory of its own making and its own earlier stages. At the present stage of its development it has taken pictures of a house and a boat and these have coagulated into parts of the mechanism. The film rolls onto the floor as more pictures are taken.

Whirlpool—Eye of the Storm., 1973 (p. 85), seems to allude to an obscure strain of spirituality within the work. A skywriting plane drew a tight spiral that was intended to go from sky to earth as a connecting channel, but which was truncated when the pilot got dizzy. It hovers elusively over genres. Incorporating the festivity of the air show or carnival, it also be-speaks the solemnity of an apparition. As painting it is ephemeral, dispersing like mist. As sculpture it is immaterial and out of reach, yet visible. As sign it is merely indefinite. As icon it resonates with the Transfiguration, the channel between above and below, the Shekinah, and the descent of Zeus upon Danaë in a cloud.

1. Oppenheim characteristically, up to the present day, refers to his work as a residue rather than as the very thing intended. One should compare Yves Klein's description of his physical works as "the ashes of my art."

2. In a parody of a scientific experiment, Duchamp took three strings, each one meter long, dropped them onto a canvas on the floor from a height of one meter, and recorded the configurations in which they landed.

3. Again a characteristic of anti-Modernist work, originating in Duchamp's 1913 introduction of the aleatory into his work, more recently echoed by Klein's "painting," in 1961, made by strapping a gessoed canvas to the roof of his car and driving from Paris to Nice in a rainstorm. These trends worked themselves out in parallel forms in Europe and America, although generally the mood assumed in the European works was more metaphysical, while in the American works it was more materialistic. Oppenheim's work, in this way, is somewhat between the two extremes.

4. *Dennis Oppenheim, Retrospective, Works 1967-1977/Dennis Oppenheim: Retrospective de l'oeuvre 1967-1977* (Montreal: Musée d'art contemporaine, 1978), p. 53.

5. This work also presaged works by Marina Abramovich and Ulay, among others, that involved relating to snakes in close bodily proximity in a gallery space.

6. The awkwardness of it is the remarkable thing; the awkwardness of Joseph Beuys lying on the floor, of Marina Abramovic and Ulay crawling around on the floor making eye contact with a snake, and so on.

7. *Dennis Oppenheim: Retrospective*, p. 62.

8. Ibid., p. 67.

9. Ibid.

10. Janet Kardon, *Machineworks: Vito Acconci, Alice Aycock, Dennis Oppenheim* (Philadelphia: Institute of Contemporary Art, 1981), p. 7.

11. Nehama Guralnik, "From Factories to Fireworks—Technology as a Poetic Extension of the Mind in the Work of Dennis Oppenheim," in *Dennis Oppenheim: Factories, Fireworks 1979-84* (Tel Aviv: The Tel Aviv Museum, 1984), pp. 7, 9.

12. Ibid., p. 13.

13. Steven Poser, "Dennis Oppenheim: The Fugitive Image," in *Dennis Oppenheim* (Geneva: Galerie Eric Franck, 1984), p. 67.

14. Ibid., p. 68.

15. See Tricia Collins and Richard Milazzo, "Behind the Eight Ball with Dennis Oppenheim," in *Dennis Oppenheim, Recent Works* (Brussels: Liverpool Gallery, 1990).

16. Ibid.

17. Ibid.

18. Stuart Morgan, "Dennis Oppenheim: Gut Reaction," *Artscribe*, Spring 1979.

Color Application for Chandra, 1971.
Installation. Harkus Krakow Gallery, Boston.
Tape loop, slide system, colored gels,
amplifier, speakers, yellow-headed parrot.
  "My two-and-a-half-year-old daughter is
taught seven basic colors by repeated exposure to projected light and to my voice. In
three hours she is able to associate the color
symbol with the word symbol, thereby acquir-
ing this data. Individual tape loops of
Chandra's voice repeating the color names
are played twenty four hours a day to a parrot
in a separate room. The parrot eventually
learns to mimic the color names. Here, color
is not directly applied to a surface, but trans-
mitted (abstracted from its source) and used
to structure the vocal responses of a bird. It
becomes a method for me to throw my
voice." (D.O.)

Gingerbread Man, 1970-71. Performance and installation. Françoise Lambert Gallery, Milan. Gingerbread man, micro-projectors, color slides of sample feces at 3000 X magnification, 8mm technicolor film loop, projector.

"A symbolic human form is subjected to the linearity of the digestive track and broken down by the activation of the digestive process. The gingerbread man is used to fill an internal space, and its process of change is linked to a life-sustaining interaction." (D.O.)

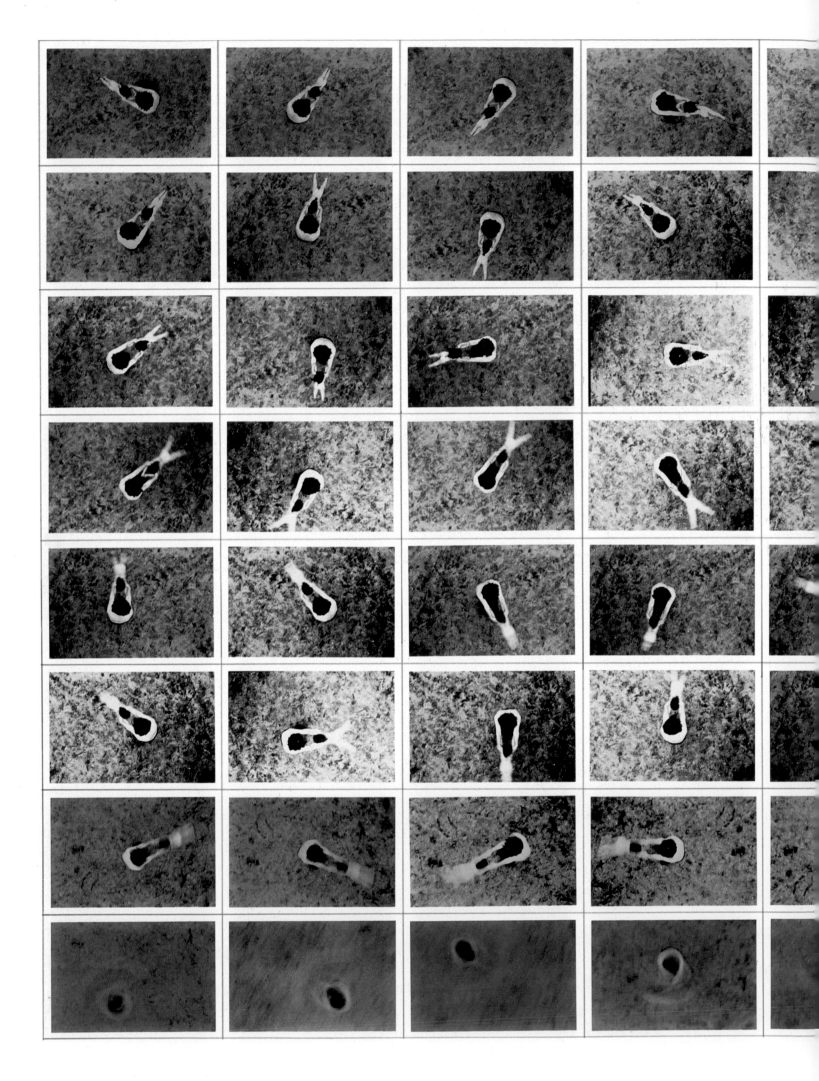

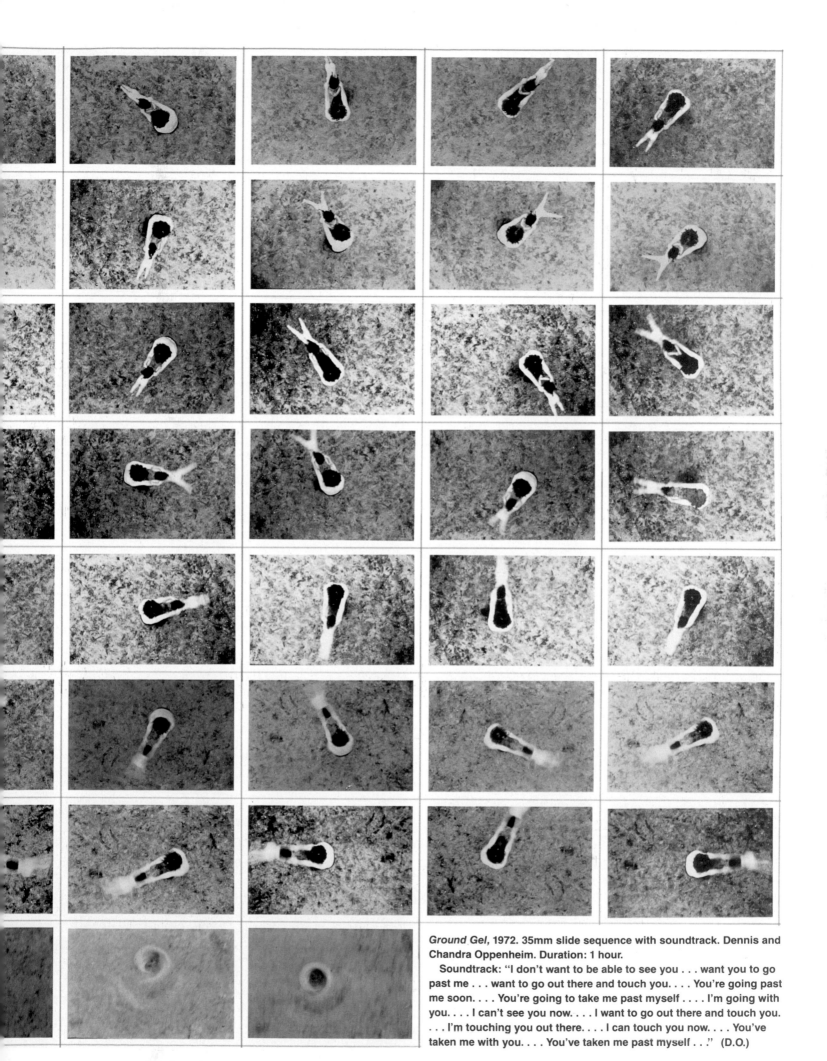

Ground Gel, 1972. 35mm slide sequence with soundtrack. Dennis and Chandra Oppenheim. Duration: 1 hour.

Soundtrack: "I don't want to be able to see you . . . want you to go past me . . . want to go out there and touch you. . . . You're going past me soon. . . . You're going to take me past myself . . . . I'm going with you. . . . I can't see you now. . . . I want to go out there and touch you. . . . I'm touching you out there. . . . I can touch you now. . . . You've taken me with you. . . . You've taken me past myself . . ." (D.O.)

Polarities, 1972. Bridgehampton, New York. Red magnesium flares. Each 500′ long.
  Top: what is presumed to be the last graphic gesture by David Oppenheim, the artist's father, before his death on November 28, 1971, enlarged and plotted with magnesium flares. *Bottom:* one of the first drawings by the artist's daughter, Chandra, enlarged and plotted with magnesium flares.

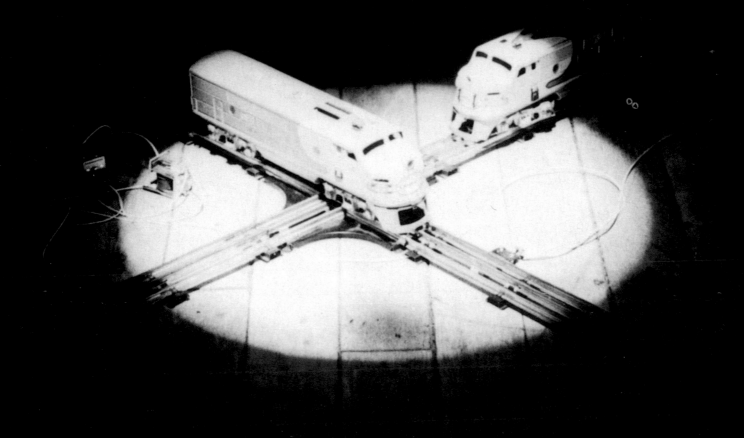

Predictions, 1972. Installation. Two electric
train sets, spotlight, colored gel. 1′ × 10′ × 10′.
   "The track section in a red spotlight is a
surrogate for an existing track located
between Syosset and Huntington at the
Amott signal on the Long Island Railroad.
This section was concentrated upon until I
could easily produce a mental picture of it.
This image is mentally superimposed onto
the surrogate track, during the prediction of a
collision date. The model trains pass this in-
tersection five-hundred times per day, two-
hundred and fifty times as frequently as the
Long Island Railroad's daily crossing. The installation will be activated at every opportunity, for as long a period as possible,
during this, and subsequent exhibitions, until
11:22 pm on June 10, 1988." (D.O.)

Opposite: 2000′ Shadow Projection, 1972.
Activity. Batavia, New York. Carbon search
arc lamp, trumpet. Duration: 1 hour.
   "The carbon arc cuts through space like a
laser, producing a cylinder of white light,
bleaching the turf. My head blocks light, producing an image in negative . . . accelerating
down the two-thousand-foot channel via two
dark parallel lines. As I blow into a horn, the
sensation of being in two places at once
takes hold. The project is executed in memory of my father, David Oppenheim." (D.O.)

This page: Whirlpool—Eye of the Storm, 1973.
El Mirage Dry Lake, Southern California.
Aircraft, smoke. ¾ × 4 miles. Duration: 1 hour.
   Directed by radio instructions from the
ground, a pilot traces the schema of a tornado with the standard white smoke dis-
charged by the aircraft.

Wishing Well, 1973. Installation. Conveyor belt, pennies, ceramic well, water, tape deck, amplifier, speakers. 2′ × 10′ × 3′.

Soundtrack: "I want to be able to sink downward. . . . I wish I could do this. . . . I want this well to act in favor of this . . . . I wish these pennies could act as sparks, to charge the eventuality of this. I know where I want to stand. I know the location to be in this city, nearby. I'll stand there as often as I can. It's not far away. My shoulder blades will be pressing against a building, a thick wall. I'll be looking out towards the street. The heels of my shoes will be pressed against the concrete and planted firmly on the sidewalk. It's not as if this material begins to soften or relax, but the first sensation is similar to that. I can feel the pavement begin to surround the soles of my shoes. At the same time, my shoulder blades have gone at least one inch back, as my feet are further engulfed by the concrete. I can feel my shoulders dragging downward, as they sink deeper into the wall. My feet are now in the pavement, not quite up to the beginning of my ankles. At this point I gently rest my head back toward the wall. As I do this the lower part of my back begins to touch the surface. My shoulders are sinking further back. The ground is well over my ankles now. I know the soles of my shoes are touching the dirt surface, four inches below the concrete slab. My body now distinguishes between the materials encroaching upon it. The sidewalk slab becomes a template passing up my leg— when it reaches my kneecaps—my feet have easily adjusted to the dirt around them, my legs are surrounded, my shoulders and much of my head have passed through the surface. I can feel the pressure moving to the front of my body, my neck is practically engulfed now, only my chin remains. My thighs are well into the ground, my feet passing through different forms of rock and gravel, dampness. My chest and stomach become the only visible portions, as the sidewalk surface is now level with my waist. My back is arched, my head well into the wall and now passing through a series of steel members. Only a small part of my stomach remains, acting as a connector between the wall and ground. My upper extremities are continuing to sink downward even though I have been pressing backward. I am now through this surface, continuing along its length, depositing the pennies into a receptacle at the end. Then in an almost vertical direction. My back is straight, arms against my sides. The material surrounding me feels of a consistent nature. . . . I don't remember it changing as I continue in this direction." (D.O.)

Recall, 1974. Color video monitor, videotape, metal pan, ink, turpentine. 1′ × 8′ × 2′.

   "As my senses are filled with smell, my memory slowly uncovers images of a past region in which the smell prevailed . . . a paint medium, when applied differently, can still be said to be accomplishing a similar result . . . instead of thinning down pigment, I'm absorbing the material into my sensory system and thinning out layers of repressed memory." (D.O.)

Soundtrack: "California . . . my first year of school . . . I remember Harry Krell's painting class. Beginning painting . . . September 19th, 1958. I was a sophomore. . . . I remember he asked us to paint . . . to paint a head . . . a male head . . . and a torso. We had a male model. I remember what the room was like . . . I remember the smell, I couldn't do what he wanted us to do. He was asking us to use warm and cool colors in juxtaposition . . . Using these colors in blocks to form contours of the head and torso . . . he didn't want us to use lines . . . just these colors . . . I remember I couldn't do this . . . advancing and receding colors . . . I remember I couldn't do this . . . I couldn't understand this . . . But I remember some of the work. I worked on this for a long time . . . I had difficulty in that class. I remember how full these classes were . . . how hard it was to find a space to put your easel and drawing board. It was on the third floor of a building. I remember walking . . . walking up there. I remember the fire escape where I used to sit and smoke. I remember some of the students . . . tying to remember their work . . . can't remember what I did. I remember Mr. Borge's drawing class . . . remember we called that class "drawing orientation" . . . the same year, 1958. California College of Art and Crafts. I remember the rendering projects . . . perspective projects . . . the excursions . . . going to the Oakland Hills and the cemetery and sketching. Mr. Post's watercolor class. We were all stimulated to paint like him. I remember being able to do that. I guess my oil painting class was most difficult. I remember after this project . . . with the head and torso we were told we could do something less restrained . . . We could just try and paint . . . without instruction . . . without guidelines . . . he would come by and discuss what we had done. I remember the figure drawing with Harry Krell again . . . the same year 1958. I had him for two classes . . . I couldn't follow his classroom assignments . . . I did things on my own that made him take notice . . . made him at least acknowledge who I was . . . he used to come behind me while I was drawing the figure . . . intrude and make corrections . . . I remember liking this class but I was a little afraid of not meeting his expectations . . . I remember one guy drawing an imitation of an exterior building . . . this is again my sophomore year which I . . ." (D.O.)

Radicality, 1974. Long Island, New York. Red, yellow, and green
strontium nitrate flares. 15′ × 100′.

Untitled Performance, 1974. Installation. The
Clocktower Gallery, New York City. Dog,
electric organ, graphite. Duration: 6 hours.
  A dead German shepherd is pulled in a spiral pattern across a floor covered with graphite. The dog's body, placed on top of an
electric organ, plays a continuous chord that
gradually changes as rigor mortis sets in,
and as the body slowly shifts.

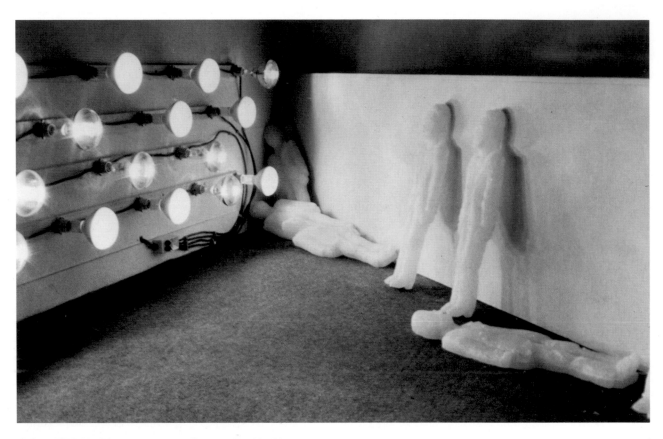

Aging, 1974. Heat lamps, cast wax figures. 3′ × 8′ × 8′.

Opposite: Rehearsal for Five Hour Slump, 1973.
Performance. Chandra Oppenheim, electric organ.
Duration: 2 hours.
   "This piece acts as a rehearsal for a performance last-
ing five hours, in which a static body produces a modu-
lated electronic sound by assuming a position on top of
the keyboard of an electric organ. Ideally it asks that the
figure dies on top of the organ. Continuous sound produced by a dead organism." (D.O.)

Attempt to Raise Hell, 1974. Cast aluminum figure, bell, felt suit, wooden base. 6′ × 4′ × 3′.
 A timing mechanism forces the figure to lunge forward and repeatedly smash its head into a bell every sixty seconds.

This page: Theme For a Major Hit, 1974.
24″-tall motor-driven marionette, 2-hour
recording, circular stage, spotlight, tape
recorder. external speakers, soundtrack.
    The marionette, a surrogate for the artist,
performs a redundant song and dance as a
soundtrack continuously plays, "It ain't what
you make, it's what makes you do it."

Opposite page: Table Piece, 1975. Two cast
figures equipped with audio synchronized
jaw movements, felt suits, wood and formica
table, audio tape. 2′ × 60′ × 2′.
    Two figures are seated at opposite ends of
a table segmented into gradations of black,
grey, beige, and white tones. Both face micro-
phones and have a dialogue across the table,
which is based on a transfer of personality
from a black to a white figure.

Lecture #1, 1976. Installation. Framartstudio, Naples. Two cast figures equipped with audio-synchronized jaw movement, felt suits, wood chairs, wood and formica lectern, audio tape. 30″ × 264″ × 446″.

In the installation, a surrogate for the artist delivers an art history lecture taking place in the 1990. Beginning with the death of Robert Smithson in 1971, he speculates on a rash of artists's assassinations. The lecturer predicts the emergence of painters of the 1980s and the deterioration of Soho in the 1990s, resulting in the demise of the avant-garde art world.

Mind Twist—Wandering, 1975. Installation.
One video monitor with an image of a
spinning head, the second with an image of a
hand slap, two electric turntables, black
sand, audio track.

Soundtrack: "Perhaps I should have stayed on that road—that road back there—see it—see how it was crossed over . . . Double-crossed in two places . . . I made a detour—changed direction. Why did I feel a curve coming, it was a straight course. But I made a slight turn, the movement was circular — each operation destroying the preceding one.

And that land . . . all that land ahead of me, finally got to actual space—actual time. I let it attack me—overpower me—I let it turn myself in on myself. First twist, the detour that started this continued, circular path—this road that goes nowhere . . . How I remember that feeling—that temptation to twist my mind—to twist my thoughts around—I'm sure it's like committing murder, because I know that it takes a twisted mind—a mind that can turn against itself . . . to stay on this

course. I wanted to show you straight, clear lines by now—all this travelling—I wanted you to look down a clear road and see the beginning and the end; to show you a thought well travelled in space—but I'm showing you this, as it is, I want you to see what takes a twisted mind to recognize." (D.O.)

Identity Stretch, 1970-75. Artpark, Lewiston, New York. Ink, thumbprints, elastic, wood, rope, hot tar, spray truck, aircraft. 300′ × 1000′.

Overlapping, inked thumbprints on an elastic band are stretched and plotted on a grid. The grid and thumbprints are transferred to an outdoor site, where a spray truck follows the line of the prints (*upper left:* Erik Oppenheim's right thumb; *right:* Dennis Oppenheim's right thumb). The work is then photographed from an aircraft.

Star Skid, 1977. Model for a project proposed for the western United States. Cast concrete, broken glass. 30′ in diameter, 200′ trench.

Tank Skid, 1977. Model for a project proposed for the western United States. Four cast concrete towers. 10′, 20′, 30′, 50′ height of each tower.

Wishing the Mountains Madness, 1977.
Missoula, Montana. 4′ × 4′ painted wooden
stars covering a 4-acre site.
    The expansive, unbounded sky contrasts
the limits and boundaries imposed by
madness.

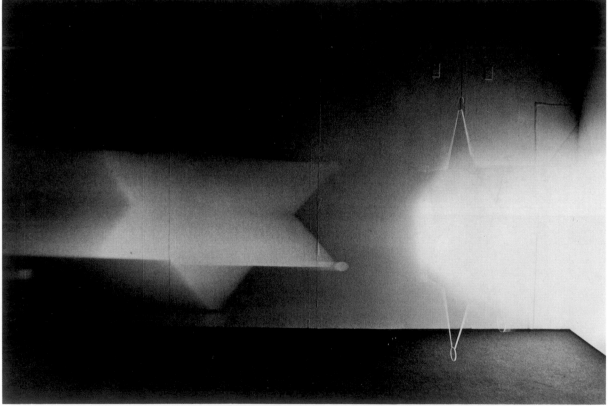

Opposite page: I Shot The Sheriff, 1977. Installation. Double barrel shotgun, electrical conduit, acrylic, turntable, spotlight, audio system.

A metallic sheriff's badge, symbolizing authority, is made large and transparent. The shotgun (barrel extended and aimed at the badge) is imperceptible in darkness, illuminated only by the reflection of the suspended badge as it moves across the gallery walls. The soundtrack is a repeat loop of Bob Marley singing: "I shot the sheriff, but I did not shoot the deputy."

Below: Early Morning Blues, 1977. 5′ diameter fully-tracked aluminum record, phase shifter, stereo amplifier, 10′ diameter neon hot plate with white enamel pot, four-channel audio track.

The oversized, spinning record, its needle stuck on a groove, makes a screeching noise while a soundtrack refers to an idea existing on the outer edge of the burner, that is, in formation in the mind.

Three Downward Blows. (Knuckle Marks)., 1977. Lolo, near Missoula, Montana. Black powder.

Explosions detonated five to six feet below the ground produce craters that measure from four to ten feet in diameter. The explosions leave impressions resembling knuckle marks on the earth.

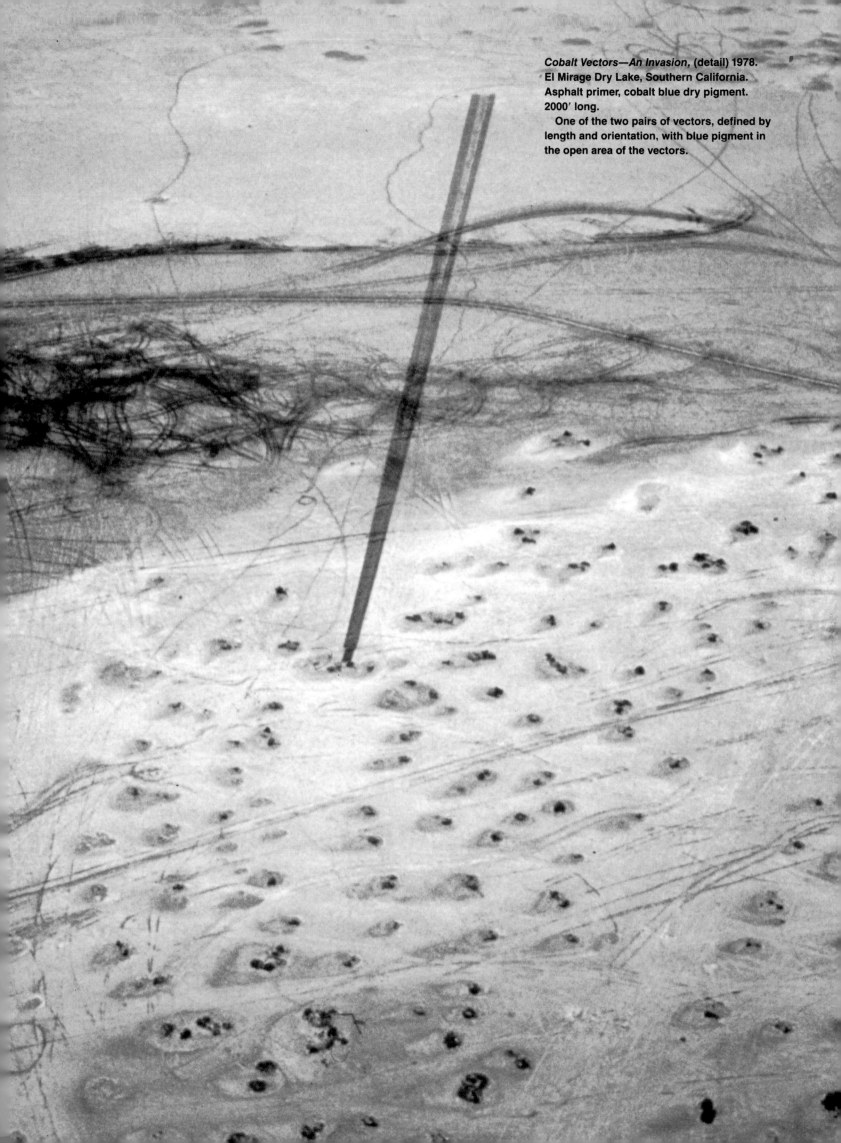

Cobalt Vectors—An Invasion, (detail) 1978.
El Mirage Dry Lake, Southern California.
Asphalt primer, cobalt blue dry pigment.
2000′ long.
    One of the two pairs of vectors, defined by
length and orientation, with blue pigment in
the open area of the vectors.

Falling Room, 1979. Aluminum frame attached to the facade of 356 West Broadway, New York City, motor with timing system. 14′ × 16′ × 50′.

A motorized "room" is raised slowly up a fifty-foot aluminum shaft. When it reaches the top, it is held for several seconds. Then, guided by a cable, the "room" falls through the shaft.

Champagne House, 1979. Solid glass blocks, cable, spotlight. 14″ × 16″ × 20″.

The solid glass house is suspended ten feet above the floor by a thin steel cable. An ellipsoidal spotlight reflects its shape on a wall.

Exit for the South Bronx, 1979. Scale model for the South Bronx, New York. Wood, fiberglass, steel, masonite. 60″ × 240″.

A spiral ramp descends from a window cut in a temporary wall. If built on a site in the South Bronx, the window would be on the second floor of an actual facade and the ramp would be on a vacant lot.

Jailbreak, 1979. Wood, fiberglass, steel, netting, ivory, arc light. 14′ × 50′ × 40′.

A statement carved on ivory plaques, that are placed on the wall reads: "It must have been his last thought that fractured these walls . . . a rambling, unfixed, multi-dimensional force . . . the shape of which could only be guessed at by the effects on obstacles in its path . . ." (D.O.)

Shape Transmission Chamber for the Ultimate Smoke Signal, 1979. Steel, wood, fiberglass. 3′ × 12′ × 2′.
 Smoke stacks are equipped with flues to regulate smoke emissions from a central chamber.

Waiting Room for the Midnight Special.
(A Thought Collision Factory for
Ghost Ships)., 1979. Scale model
for Sand Point, Seattle. Excavated earth,
concrete, wood, steel, fiberglass.
1′ × 20′ × 10′.

Opposite page: Scan, 1979. Installation.
Württembergischer Kunstverein Stuttgart.
Wood, steel, two electric skeet machines,
clay discs. 20′ × 80′ × 80′.
  Two standard commercial machines that
automatically fire clay pigeons are positioned
behind shields *(this page)* at opposite cor-
ners of a room. The arms of the machines are
adjusted to allow the projected discs to collide or pass through a ring in the middle of
the room. The installation is a scale model
proposal for an underground site, using two
concrete tunnels, where the top of the ring
would correspond to the only visible part of
the site piece. From this point, the viewer
would be able to scan the collision of the
automatically fired discs. The discs are
meant as physical metaphors for projected
thought.

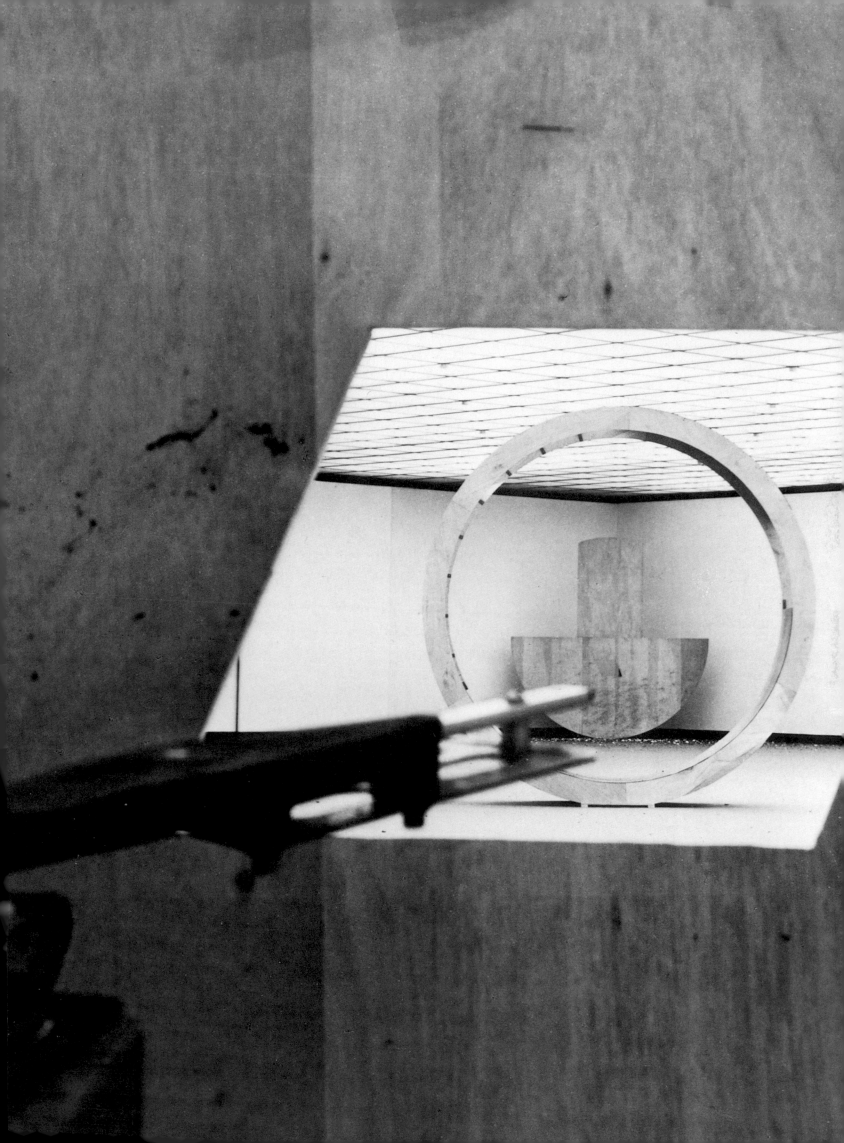

Way Station Launching an Obsolete Power.
(A Thought Collision Factory in Pursuit of
Journey). (A Clip in a Rifle Weapon)., 1979.
Wood, fiberglass, rubber, cables, turbine
ventilator, air ducts, conveyor belt,
centrifugal blowers. 9′ × 14′ × 30′.

Diamond Cutter's Wedding, 1979. High-powered butane heater, wood, fiberglass, steel, wire mesh, pendulum, cord, pulleys, netting. 13' × 50' × 12'. *This page:* rear view. *Opposite page, top:* Drawing, 1979. Pencil, colored pencil, oil wash on paper. 38" × 50". *Bottom:* side view.

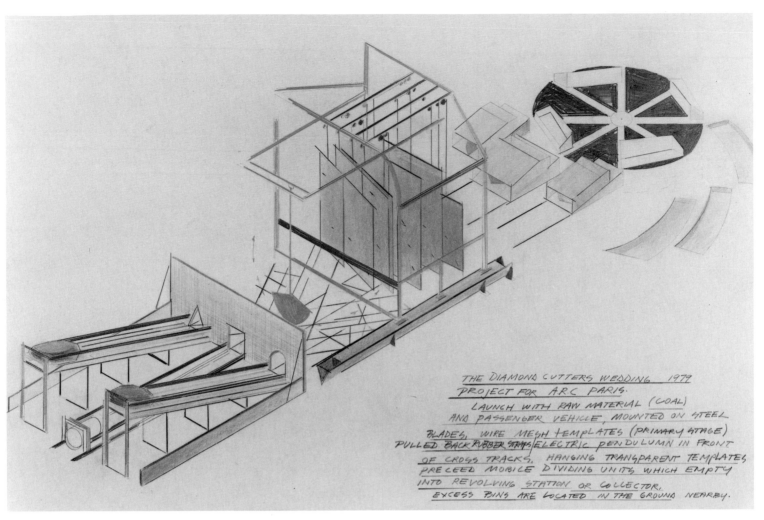

THE DIAMOND CUTTERS WEDDING   1979
PROJECT FOR A.R.C. PARIS.
LAUNCH WITH RAW MATERIAL (COAL)
AND PASSENGER VEHICLE, MOUNTED ON STEEL
BLADES, WIRE MESH TEMPLATES (PRIMARY STAGE)
PULLED BACK RUBBER STRAPS, ELECTRIC PENDULUMN IN FRONT
OF CROSS TRACKS, HANGING TRANSPARENT TEMPLATES
PRECEED MOBILE DIVIDING UNITS WHICH EMPTY
INTO REVOLVING STATION OR COLLECTOR,
EXCESS BINS ARE LOCATED IN THE GROUND NEARBY.

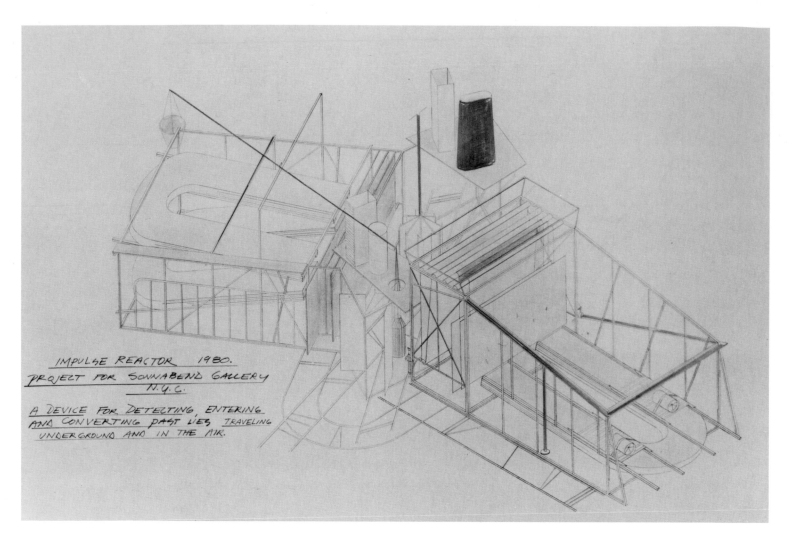

IMPULSE REACTOR 1980.
PROJECT FOR SONNABEND GALLERY
N.Y.C.

A DEVICE FOR DETECTING, ENTERING
AND CONVERTING PAST LIES TRAVELING
UNDERGROUND AND IN THE AIR.

Top: Impulse Reactor. A Device for Detecting, Entering, and Converting Past Lies Travelling Underground and in the Air., 1980. Pencil, colored pencil, oil wash on paper. 38″ × 50″.

Left: Caged Vacuum Projectiles, 1979. Scale model. Exchange-shape transmission chambers, steel smokestacks, vacuum cleaners, rubber straps, formed wooden suction units. 4′ × 7′ × 21′.

Opposite page, top left: Saturn Up-Draft, (detail) 1979. Wire mesh, wood, steel, rock, butane heater, fiberglass, rotating motor, induction fan. 20′ × 22′ × 45′.

Opposite page, top right: Revenge, 1979. Steel, galvanized steel, wood, fiberglass, extension ladder, garden tools, bench, rubber straps, steel jacks, plaster chicken wire, conveyor belt. 15′ × 14′ × 40′.

Opposite page, bottom: Crystal Recorder. (Stroking the Throat of Tornado Diane). An Early Warning System., 1980. Pencil, colored pencil, oil wash, oil pastel on paper. 50″ × 77″.

10' X 9' X 10'
CHRYSTALS, KEYS, WEIGHTS,
CONIC PAN, FORMICA.

STUDY FOR: CHRYSTAL
RECORDER. (STROKING
THE THROAT OF TORNADO
DIANE) PROJECT FOR
UNIVERSITY OF CALIF AT IRVIN
COPPER, WOOD, MOTORS, PULLEYS, SPINNING
PANS, GLASS ROD — AN EARLY WARNING SYSTEM

Dennis Oppenheim 1980.

The Assembly Line. (With By-Products from a Mechanical Trance)., 1980. High-powered blowers, vents, suspended tables, motorized metronome, fan supported by overhead boom, transparent air sacs on rotary rack, mobile shields with springs between plates, hatch openings into stage deck.
14′ × 75′ × 33′.

"Within an industrial assembly line, air-filled aerial sacs issue from a ceiling-mounted revolving conveyor belt. These forms are by-products of a machine that has hypnotized itself; its inner workings have bred solid forms of mechanical hysteria.

These air-filled transparent breaths are internal evidence of a mechanical language voicing itself through a physical by-product." (D.O.)

Station for Detaining and Blinding Radioactive Horses, 1981-82. Steel, galvanized steel, rubber strap, wire mesh, stacks, vents, pulleys, counterweights, excavated pits, boom, templates, canvas. 25′ × 100′ × 250′.

Final Stroke. Project for a Glass Factory., 1980. Steel, glass, rubber straps, pulleys, grinding wheels, galvanized stacks, electric motors, vacuum cleaners, gasoline-powered heater. 16′ × 60′ × 35′.

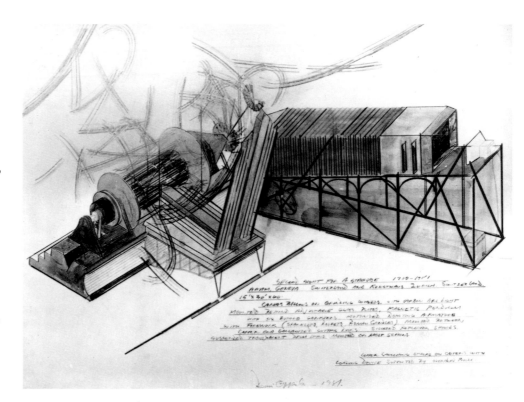

Opposite page: Life Support System for a Premature By-Product. (From a Long Distance)., (detail) 1981. Canvas, glass, steel, pulleys, wood, cloth, wire, cymbals, felt, conveyor belt, steel mesh, wire mesh, glass, rubber hose, acrylic tube, acrylic connectors, jacks, springs, induction fan. 12′ × 80′ × 40′.

This page, top: Second Sight for a Staircase. (From the Fireworks Series)., 1981. Pencil, colored pencil, oil wash, oil pastel on paper. 38″ × 50″. *Bottom: Second Sight for a Staircase. (From the Fireworks Series).*, (detail) 1981. Canvas bellows, grinding wheels, carbon arc lights, glass plates, steel frame, magnetic pendulum, butane canisters, rotating armature, sparklers, rockets, Roman candles, galvanized reflector shields, mesh screens, cutting discs, transparent drum skins, overhead boom, wood, fiberglass. 15′ × 60′ × 30′.

Launching Structure #2. (An Armature for Projection). (From the Fireworks Series)., 1981-82. Butane gas ignition system on mobile towers. Spinning glass rods, rockets, copper ricochet shields on casters with blue glass windows, galvanized cooling bin, copper recording plate, hanging diamond plate, vibrating platform with suspended black light. Eight-foot-diameter curved glass arcs with rockets, rolling glass ball with fuse, carbon arc light, revolving wheels with fountains and rockets turning a steel disc with butane torch, hanging tambourine with four spinning blades. Mobile kaleidoscope. 14′ × 60′ × 75′.

ANOTHER POINT OF ENTRY: AN INTERVIEW WITH DENNIS OPPENHEIM
Alanna Heiss

AH Dennis, we're going to conduct a series of taped discussions. Information of more than a personal or idiosyncratic interest will be transcribed. But we have to have some ground rules. An agreed-upon vocabulary.

DO I'm not sure.

AH For instance, we have to divide up areas of your work, sometimes chronologically, and give them labels. Then I will ask you questions about a particular category.

DO I'd rather not think of my work divided up like a cheese board.

AH That's too bad. Think of it like botany. Pretend you're a plant.

DO That's easy. What categories are you thinking of?

AH Just the normal ones—Earth Art, Conceptual Art, Body Art, Machine Art, and so on.

DO What's the problem?

AH I just don't want to waste time fidgeting with categorical nomenclature, instead of learning more about your work.

DO It could be arranged another way.

AH Materials? Travel schedules? Geographical? Color?

DO Never mind. Categories.

AH OK.

DO OK.

AH You've been called a Conceptual artist. But Dennis, what does that really mean?

DO My work comes from an idea, and therein lies its conceptual aspect. But it's not the only root. You know, concepts always seem to be cerebral activities, located in the mind. But why not locate them in the stomach, the gut? Much of my work comes from the "eye of the gut." It's not mental, not visual, but somewhere in between.

AH Even now, you are referred to as a Conceptual artist, probably because the term is a nice big umbrella. Since you do so many different kinds of work, maybe it's the single idea that the public can pin on you—conceptual, as in thought.

DO Yes, deranged thought. Thought as in pressure. I'm aware of a pressure, but again it comes from the middle; it's as if the eye/mind locates itself in the mid-section of the body.

AH Maybe, but a functioning brain lies behind it all, and it's clear to me that your work is not primarily linguistically based.

DO No, language is only one ingredient; in a recipe, language is the flour you add to the water or it can be the water you add to the flour. In other words, it's as if you're at the starting line, and the gun goes off. The idea goes off. It could start with a word that creates an image or with an image that creates a word. But it's the race, or the activity of finishing, that one is engaging. These constructs move from one place to another while your mind is running. At the end it shouldn't matter what structure is being used. By then it's pure mental adrenaline, which has its own laws and logic, and that's as it should be. One is enraptured by trusting something beyond control. In this sense, I don't think visually.

AH Isn't, "I don't think visually," a provocative statement for one of the world's important artists to make?

DO Obviously, I have a little trouble with Formalism, even though there is a state of mind I can

Formula Compound. A Combustion Chamber. An Exorcism. (From the Fireworks Series)., 1982.
Activation at the State University of New York at Potsdam.

synthetically create that allows me to get close to Formalist thinking. I can trick myself into thinking that the pursuit of such a direction could be legitimate. I can even understand how a person might pursue such a direction for his or her lifetime.

AH Let's compare you and James Turrell. Both of you use the vocabulary of an installation artist. Both of you work with projects that are long-range, exhausting, even visionary. But Turrell seems, in the context of this discussion, to be more involved with perceptual matters, much as a painter would be—with format and light and shadow. He shapes our sense of color.

DO Turrell comes from phenomenology and visual perception. You could say he's doing better monochromatic painting with the sky than many monochromatic painters are doing on canvas. The work seduces you, and you go along with it. You tend not to question him to the extent you might other Formalist painters.

AH Let's talk about your early pieces, where ideas were more important than seduction, more vital than visuals. *Annual Rings*, 1968 (pp. 24-25) and *Landslide*, 1968 (pp. 18-19), have a quasi-scientific quality to them, which seems to be at odds with what feels like the old-fashioned notion of the artist immersing himself in nature. In a 1968 article on earthworks, Sidney Tillam speculated about Earth Art as a "picturesque quest," as a substitution of sentimentality for nobility of feeling, the cult of nature as an anecdote for excessive cultural sophistication.

DO Well, this notion of the artist immersing himself in nature—the theory of the picturesque—was not part of the recipe of entry that concerned all Earth artists. Only a few of them have had a dialogue with this idea, perhaps Richard Long and some other English artists. My use of quasi-scientific nuance or notation was meant to oppose abstract gestures on the land, lines that only meant themselves and didn't refer to anything else. I believed applying abstract gesture onto the land was carrying a studio ideology that referred to painting, out of doors. It was retrograde. If you were going to use land, you should make it part of a holistic, ecological, geological, anthropological continuum.

So when I did lines on the snow, lines which came from a map, I referred to them as information lines. They may have looked like abstract gestures, even Abstract Expressionist gestures, but the intent was to suture the work with lines or notations that had larger fields of association. Lines could mean rainfall or temperature. I was not paying attention to the picturesque as a possibility. I used terms like "studio organism"; quasi-ecological terms that were meant to contrast studio habits with exterior habits or habitats. I took my clues from ecology, pushing towards what the critic Jack Burnham called "real time systems." A sculptor in real time systems wouldn't want studio references to bleed into the land. He would want to have a new dialogue with the external site.

AH So, if you weren't searching out locations because they were beautiful or interesting to you, how would you determine where you would do an Earth Art piece for example? Why choose exit 52 on the Long Island Expressway for *Landslide*?

DO I was drawn to ravaged sites. When I wanted to undertake a piece, I would go to New Jersey and stomp around chemical dumps. This was one of the reasons why it was difficult to do earthworks under the jurisdiction of a planned exhibition. Sites were places that had not been incorporated into a system—dumps, borders of countries, deserts, and waste lands—peripheries. If the land wasn't degenerate enough for me, I'd write words like "diphtheria" on the hillside. The idea was a severe disjuncture from the pastoral.

AH There was another reason why many people got involved in old locations, like strip mine sites. They were simply more available; it was easier to arrange the kind of pieces we are talking about in a place no one cared about, than to run a motorcycle around Central Park in a giant circle, destroying a lot of grass. Certainly as an organizer of installations and exhibitions, this was apparent to me. I asked

Robert Smithson about the issue of convenience as a factor in site selection just before he did the strip-mining projects. He agreed it was certainly easier to grab large areas of rejected land, but suggested that artists's greed for space and convenience was a minor factor. The more important consideration was an artistic and aesthetic corrective that sought to transform land made ugly and useless by human activity. It was about something good and wonderful being done by a human on land that another human had made bad or useless. We also discussed how there was an economic, industrial-art symmetry in this idea that could turn dangerously into self-righteousness.

DO I think Smithson identified with the problem of the morality of the ideal. There were artists who immediately picked up on that notion and began to execute works that took a moral position, rectifying pathological evils. But this was clearly a pulled punch that did not allow for a work to transcend itself. Directing a work towards a moral position is often a weakness. It steals the presumed power from a collected consciousness that tries to fill a space left by a lack of invention.

AH But Tillam also implied that you guys were all kidding. Instead of staring at the sunset and sighing, you were taking a chain saw and cutting a hole in the ground and looking at the sunset and sighing. So you were doing basically the same thing.

DO Well, one has to come to grips with what amount of the gesture went towards the site and what amount didn't have anything to do with it. A good part of the thinking could have been supplanted to objects or non-objects or dematerialized states, not locations. There are Earth artists who have only focused on a very specific formal treatment for twenty-five years. Clearly, a large percentage of their momentum was already monomaniacal at the time.

For me, Earth Art was already decompartmentalized and splitting apart as I was doing it. It quickly whiplashed into what was diametrically opposed to it—Body Art. I knew that I could have gotten another ten years out of making inscriptions in the ground before they would start to wear thin. I also knew I would have trouble justifying such a monodirectional pursuit. I wasn't looking for the Earth Art to give way, and Body Art to take over; I was looking for a kind of hybrid unbeknownst to me. It was like mixing your own chemistry as you're thinking. Mixing liquids in your own system, not knowing the exact outcome.

AH Was your Earth and Body Art an extension, or a denunciation, of the influence of Minimalism on art in the late 1960s and 1970s?

DO Conceptual Art, by and large, was in a dialogue with Minimalism, and was literally descended from Minimalism through its practitioners. They retain a dialogue to this day. In fact, the earthworks you see now that are done by the classic practitioners are either a continuation of this original position or a degeneration rising out of sheer fatigue from the distance they've gone. That's one of the problems with Formalism; a fatigue factor registers in the work.

AH Was your work an extension or a denunciation?

DO The urge was to go beyond Minimalism. It was clear, even to the Minimalists, that their idea was reaching ground zero. That's why phenomenology became a way of expanding the domain—and a valid way at that. We know that Minimalism quickly lifted off into phenomenology via the work of Bruce Nauman and Turrell and the writings of Robert Morris.

AH Dennis, how does it feel to look back on Earth and Body Art pieces that you made twenty years ago, that do not exist, except in documentation that seems so limited and in some cases inferior?

DO In 1968 and 1969 I lived in an apartment. I didn't need a studio. Everything that I had done as an artist was contained in one small case of slides. And, it accounted for two of the most strenuous years of work in my whole life. I distinctly remember realizing this while sitting and looking at virtually everything I had done.

Formula Compound. A Combustion Chamber.
An Exorcism. (From the Fireworks Series).,
1982. State University of New York at
Potsdam. Welded painted steel, perforated
steel, steel angle, pipe, channel, tube,
galvanized metal, rockets, fountains, flares.
28′ × 65′ × 50′.

Formula Compound. A Combustion Chamber. An Exorcism. (From the Fireworks Series)., 1982. Activation at "Art on the Beach," New York City.

AH Was that a sense of freedom? Or despair?

DO There are stories of Giacometti returning from a ten year trip with works that fit into a match
It's not necessarily reductive; it's simply that you are practicing what you preach, with convict
Many of my Earth Art pieces were supposed to vanish, virtually as I was building them. There
some machine pieces that were saved, but we lost a number of them. One is pulled into remorse a l
more when you lose something that is complicated.

AH Over the years pictures documenting your early work have become iconic, but what do they re
communicate about those works or about the experience of making those works to us twenty ye
later?

DO As pictures age, they remove themselves from the instant; certain things happen to the informat
in them. I've always admitted that it was necessary to make photographic documentation. It wa
naiveté that co-existed with the outdoor work.

AH In a 1968 article in *Newsweek*, there is a picture of *Landslide*, taken from the top of the hill, a
you're standing at the bottom. I looked at it and said, "Wait a minute. This makes the piece co
pletely different from the way I know it from other pictures." What really was the piece? Was it y
doing it at the time? Was the piece in your photographs? Was the piece over when you walked awa

DO The photographer who took the picture for *Newsweek* assumed a strange position on the ban
After looking through the lens he said, "I could destroy you with this shot." I realized then that we h
problems. On one hand, I knew virtually nobody was going to see *Landslide*, except the photograph
But once he clicked the shutter, millions of people were going to see the piece. So I realized th
photograph was important. As much as I may have recognized the importance of documentation, ar

Accelerator for Evil Thoughts. (From the Fireworks Series)., 1983. Pencil, colored pencil, oil wash, oil pastel on paper. 50" × 77".

even if I focused on it to the point where it fed my ideas through paranoia, I couldn't make the obsession stick. The next day I was off doing another piece, caring even less about the way it would be seen. This is the truth.

AH I know you probably wouldn't include Christo in your summary of Earth artists, but I include him. Documentation has been important to him in a way that it was never important to you or to other Earth artists. Christo controls his photographs. No photographer takes a photograph, unless Christo hires him and Christo pays him. No photograph is released to any news magazine or newspaper without Christo's approval.

DO Christo has always controlled his products.

AH I'm not criticizing you or him. I'm just pointing out that for certain artists documentation *has* been a part of their process.

DO You can't understand how strange it was to be a sculptor who exhibited photographs. You operated on truly a large scale, but when photographs represented the work everything closed down into a pictorial configuration. You were always making excuses for poor documentation, saying what you were doing was an advanced art, and there were only a few ways to communicate it. But in reality the work was gone, and there was nothing to see. That was the way I wanted it.

AH But you didn't put in the time or seriously budget the money for photography, which implies you never took documentation seriously, right?

DO Some care was given to the original documentations. It's true, one wasn't inclined to make the documentation too large, in color, or to mount them very well. It was a slapdash procedure that came from an idealistic view that one was doing these things outside and they were not controllable as images. Some of these works came to be treated respectfully as two-dimensional pictures, but the pictorial representations contradict what the actual situation was in 1967 and 1968. Museums treat artifacts and artworks the same way today; they often aggrandize them even though they might not have been grand originally. It is strange that so much second generation Conceptualism came about through a reaction to the documentation procedures of this period and not to the root activity itself. It's really a lesson in how things distort.

AH But, what *was* the piece? In your mind, did those early pieces exist beyond your original realization through documentation, however modest? For example, in my mind, Smithson's *Spiral Jetty* is just two photographs.

DO That's certainly what Baudrillard would say.

AH It's a memory to me, aided by two photographs. Not many people saw it. By the way, I have no problem with ephemeral art. Most art exists in memory aided by photographs. After all, how many times do you check in at the Prado? How many times do you actually see Bosch's paintings?

DO There's another point here, Alanna, another consideration about *Spiral Jetty* and the early Earth Art pieces. In terms of percentages, they didn't have a high visual quality. *Spiral Jetty* is seventy-five percent mental. It doesn't need pictorial differentiations. It's basically the *idea* of earthworks, the idea of the salt flats. There are millions of spiral configurations. In other words, it's about the salt, submersions, the jetty, what is around the salt flats. In the end, it's about mental configurations.

Some of my pieces, like the snow pieces, were about temperature, the fact that it was freezing. When you do a drawing of the piece, and it's freezing with a chill factor as you move a pencil across the paper, that's the idea. The visual quotient is not as strenuous as you think. What am I supposed to do? Carry around ice cubes, asking people to put their hand inside the bag?

AH Relative to painting and sculpture, it took a lot of money to make Earth Art, to get everything right. The movement took on elements of megalomania, because Earth Art involved huge areas of land, and

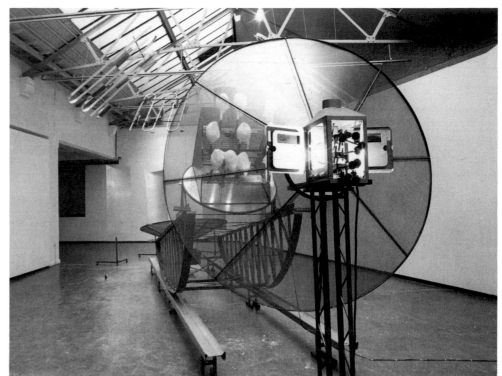

Left: Object with a Memory, 1983. Fiberglass, wood, steel, galvanized metal, aluminum, glass, copper, hand saws, casters, circular saws, auger bits, shades, plastic wire, cable, pencils, drum skins, shingles. 12′ × 8′ × 18′.

Above (top): Vibrating Forest. (From the Fireworks Series)., 1982. Steel frame, rockets mounted on hanging track, arc light, vibrating motors, cotton candy machine, gunpowder, glass rods, mesh, metal shields on casters, flares, fountains. 20′ × 10′ × 45′.

Above: Image Intervention, 1984. Steel, concrete, wood, punch plate, galvanized grating, screen, boulders, glass, painted surfaces. 26′ × 60′ × 80′.

Power Fingers, 1983. Perforated steel, steel
angles, hinges, steel springs, galvanized
metal, rockets, flares, fountains. 12′ × 18′ × 5′.

Opposite page: Model for *Newton Discovering
Gravity,* 1984. Artpark, Lewiston, New York.
Aluminum head, baked enamel, corrugated
steel, perforated steel, galvanized steel, steel
pipe, bearings, cement foundation, rockets,
flares, fountains. 24′ × 20′ diameter.

it merged with peoples's egos. Who could get the largest space, the most number of acres. First, there was the generation of artists that worked with the environment. The second generation dealt with the idea of disappearing. This idea was in Richard Long's work in the beginning. Earth Art pieces became a dialectic between disappearance and the monument. Christo's eccentric challenge was to undertake projects that were monumental in every way and completely temporal. This was in opposition to Michael Heizer, for instance, who built his city in the desert, meant to last for all of time. All these impulses were pretty deeply felt. The artist was given a chance to do something on a scale that was not only beyond a gallery or a museum, but beyond nationality. Was something to exist forever? Were these artists making drawings on such a scale that only people on other planets could become involved with them? Is that really what you were about?

DO It *was* radical, if you consider late 1967 or 1968 as the time when most of these huge pieces were done. I defend the approach of radicality, the fact that outdoor works invited a dialogue with real time in ways that art had not done before. They were a strenuous departure from the traditional art settings and contexts. Unfortunately, the work quickly became postured, a recycling of abstract sculptural idiom. In other words, it just didn't go the full nine yards. I chose a course, a diabolical act, to circumvent it. I found this other agitation, the body, and I felt that unless I gave myself the chance to pursue it, I was going to be forever disappointed. I couldn't help but stretch myself into it.

AH You undertook the Body Art as a parallel activity?

DO I started a dialogue between "land wounds" and scars on my body in works like *Land Incision*, 1968 and *Arm & Wire*, 1969 (p. 45). Then in 1969, I got video equipment, and I began to record activities. Earth Art quickly evolved into Body and Performance Art for me.

AH At this point did you have any communication with Bruce Nauman?

DO Everyone knew everyone. I met Bruce in 1970. But I knew about him before, because I'm from the West Coast where he lived.

AH He wasn't as involved in Earth Art as he was with intimate video. He was making impressions of parts of his body. Were you familiar with Nauman's *Black Balls* (1967-68) film, by the way?

DO I had seen it, definitely. Bruce and I didn't see each other that much. I was talking to Vito Acconci more, because he lived in New York. Acconci came on the scene about a year after me, I think in early 1969.

AH You and Acconci are very close; it's a famous friendship. Both of you were busy taking chances in your art and not worrying about documenting what you were up to.

DO So much energy was required to initiate the act, and when it came time to snapping the photograph, there wasn't a great deal of interest on the part of the artist. I'm speaking for myself, of course. The energy went into originating the stance, building the nerve. It was radical for an artist to partake in an art that was unfolding on a daily basis, in a drama that was constantly upping the ante. Works flirted with danger. The very matrix of the work was asking for more and more risk. Concepts were being laid, one on top of the other, in a volley that, if I had been outside of the arena, I would have been extremely uncomfortable not to participate in.

To many people, particularly in Europe, the movement was powerful. It had a currency of legitimacy, a currency of art historical lineage—the artist as instigator; the artist as victim; the artist as energy drain; the artist as target. We all know, analyzing what happened after the smoke cleared, that the form of the work was undernourished.

AH Nothing to buy. Nothing to sell. Nothing to be had. Typical Oppenheim. A lot of trouble. But you were breaking frontiers.

DO For a short period of time this was true. Everyone who practiced Earth Art, to some degree, felt this deeply. It was discovery. Treasure. Even Body Art was, in a sense, too. At the time the urgency was to touch on as many things as possible. There was a conscious state of mind in which there seemed to be many possibilities that looked as if they could qualify as legitimate art positions. Some of them were radical. We're talking about a kind of art that nourished a utopian view. And it was my first experience in the dangers of that kind of thinking. Because truly any artist who thinks he is making a breakthrough in the classic sense, beginning a new movement, is intoxicated by the density and the sheer grandeur of what he thinks he's doing. For the moment, he imagines a potency that doesn't exist. One is inclined to be a bit myopic. There is a tendency to exclude other possibilities, and in excluding them, to develop an unrealistic and imperfect grasp of what you're doing. It's a condition that happens. Artists are intoxicated by their sense of claim, and it channels them even more into a single direction. They become dogmatic.

It seems easy to defend your position and to threaten other positions of art-making. But in reality things co-exist in grandeur with other movements that are showing their head. In the middle of Earth Art, there were the seeds that would destroy it. We destroyed it ourselves. It's dangerous to let rarified oxygen overcome you.

AH Speaking of positions, I'm not comfortable positioning you as someone who cares about other people or social groups. You're more concerned about individuals. Some artists have a genuine commitment to social change. They believe their visions can have political impact. Joseph Beuys was the most obvious example. Beuys thought he might change something, and he tried to. He was important to the Green Party and a crucial teacher at the Dusseldorf Kunstakademie. He invested much of his time and energy with students. I don't sense any such inclination on your part, Dennis.

DO Very early on, when Earth Art was displayed to the art world, I was among many who were constantly asked to lecture. In 1969 I had the occasion to pose as a pathologically concerned person, a spokesperson who could have taken on more than the art context. But this seemed totally preposterous to me, because I was always too enchanted by the art context to compromise it, even though I was constantly being asked questions. Someone from the audience would say, "Well you're talking about art; we're talking about life and death." They were talking about something more important than I was, admittedly, but it was an art lecture. I mean, I'm an artist! Certainly their point was well made, but it just didn't seem to come easily to me.

Whereas Beuys took the occasion, because he had the mind and the energy and the interest. Plus, he could see that his art was carrying on a dialogue with social issues. He didn't feel such discussions could harm his art, and they really didn't, because he kept doing work. In fact, the work seemed to be almost exalted because of the messiah he had become.

AH But the issue is, who were *you* communicating to?

DO One had trouble constituting the audience in this early work. You sometimes ended up subverting the audience. You were doing something that was so dematerialized, so uncompromising. It intoxicated you, because you were getting such incredible results.

AH Are you concerned with audience at all? Do you think about the people who might see your work?

DO There is something about audience that I fundamentally don't understand. There are some artists who have a tremendous sense of the receiver in the art-making process. They figure the audience into what they do, strenuously. The context seems to be extremely pertinent to some artists in terms of their entry, in terms of their content, in terms of their substance. I've had difficulty even conjuring any sense of a target or there being anything to address to anyone. In other words, audience doesn't play into my working procedure or how I conjure a work, or how I position ideas—any of those features I describe as being preliminary to the artwork. This has been very disconcerting to me, because I know I must be

Impersonation Station, 1988. Photo etched plates, wooden and glass doors and windows, aluminum drum, rotating steel wheels, cables, steel furnaces, concrete base, topiary trees. 25′ × 60′ × 60′.

doing work to communicate. Otherwise I wouldn't do it. I know in some cases, it's extremely difficult to communicate my works, to make them visible. So, I know I am silently addressing an invisible audience, but I'm never aware of the audience controlling the work I do.

I also have very little concern or patience for any kind of deliberation of context, which is another important feature for many artists. Where the show is. What the context is. Indoors. Outdoors.

AH But you're not *oblivious* to an audience. Or are you?

DO The audience doesn't make any difference. Some of the best work I've done has been done in obscure, remote places without an audience. Some problematic work has been done knowing that there would be a considerable audience. The supposition of a large audience upsets the process. But there is nothing I can strategically muster—no additional acuity, horse sense, or strategic cushion by which to protect myself.

Often when I'm asked to do something in a public place, I find it extremely difficult. I have very little agility to do anything except what I can conjure without any sort of lead or any kind of direction. It's pretty limiting in certain respects. So you can see why it is difficult for me to operate with site-specific work bounded within a plaza, say a commission, which I sometimes get. If you want to display sensitivity, and you want to bring up in yourself some sort of vocabulary that can engage the site so the sculpture doesn't look as if it's plunked down, you have to admit that what you're gazing upon, to get this energy, is just a few walls and a fountain and a bench. It's basic, and unless you succumb to parody and satire in your work, it's going to be pretty compromising, architecturally subservient. The architects are going to make sure of this.

AH But you *do* accept public commissions.

DO I was recently asked to do a commission, an outdoor sculpture at a plaza in California. It was a typical office complex with buildings and land and tennis courts. I finally realized it was probably better for me, if I'm going to be involved at all, to give them something that I'd already done or just bow out. I felt that there's more credibility in a work that has gone through a process, than to artificially come up with something new in relation to the site. I wrote a letter explaining that anything I would conjure in a dialogue with their site would not be as good as something I *had* to make. They believed me.

AH A striking and depressing statement from you because of your participation over all these years with site-specific art. I know that no one likes the term "site-specific," but it's a useful label. Responding to a site is something you do very seriously, but you're talking about a case where the parameters are such that they become a binding force on the imagination.

DO There's a lot of pretentious ideas about site-specific work and the aura of a site. There's a good reason for looking hard at the rationale in which a site-specific work would always be better than one that has absolutely nothing to do with the site, because it was done for a different reason. There's a certain credibility attached to works that have to be in a certain site. In a way, it's like the emperor's new clothes. This aura has precipitated a lot of work subservient to the site; the site had some Zen quality. Artists felt they were quite often having a conversation with a nonexistent entity.

AH What about your early sound installations, which weren't site bound?

DO I did one, *Color Application for Chandra* in 1971 (p. 76-77) where we taught my two-and-a-half-year-old daughter, Chandra, the colors red, blue, yellow, and green by shining brightly colored lights onto snow. Then we taped her voice as she tried to repeat the colors back to us. Then we took the tape of her voice saying "yellow" and played it to a parrot who mimicked it.

AH Child abuse.

DO Child abuse, yes, but in the context of Conceptual Art, and I use that term loosely, I was teaching and implanting something onto a mind. Asking Chandra to memorize colors was a bit like painting. Color was applied to her memory track by teaching the words to her for the first time. Then we would repeat these words over the period of an hour or so, which was about the length of her attention span. Sometimes it was hard for her to tell the difference between red and pink, since we were projecting the colors on a snow. After a period of time it appeared that she had learned them, so we took a sound loop of yellow, her saying "yellow," and, of course, it was "lellow," because it was baby talk. The section was looped onto a soundtrack and then played in an installation at Harkus Krakow Gallery in Boston to a yellow-headed parrot, which is a parrot that can mimic perfectly.

One room had wall-sized gels fluttering on the screen and the soundtrack, "Chandra, what is this?" In a big room was the parrot on a beautiful perch with sound equipment, the tape loop, and a yellow florescent tube. The whole room was yellow, and the parrot was learning to say "yellow."

AH You felt you were painting on Chandra's memory?

DO Yes, in the passing of a voice from me to Chandra to the parrot. I referred to the piece as "throwing my voice." It was one of the early pieces with my children as agents in a conceptually framed, almost performance setting. I wanted to teach Chandra the colors. I rationalized or deconstructed that to mean that by teaching her, I was applying color to her memory. She would remember the colors, and I was the artist doing it. I then threw her voice to the parrot. In other words, I was throwing my voice through her mind to create the sound coming from a parrot.

DO The linkage was important.

AH Genetically.

DO Yes.

AH Did the parrot function like William Wegman's dogs?

DO Perhaps, but dogs are special; I used dogs, too, shortly after the parrot. I did an installation with twelve German shepherds, *Protection*, 1971 (pp. 63-64), in front of the Museum of Fine Arts in Boston. They were guarding an area of land around the museum, forming a barricade that visitors had to pass through in order to enter the building. Then there was a dead dog installation at The Clocktower in 1973, *Untitled Performance* (pp. 90-91). We took a dog that had just died and placed it on top of an electric organ keyboard. We got the dead dog from the American Society for the Prevention of Cruelty to Animals.

AH I may over-interpret the Clocktower piece since I produced it. But the distinguishing fact of the installation, it seemed to me at the time, was that it had to do with residual activity in the same way that Robert Morris's line drawings were residual activity, a very European notion. The idea of consequence was very important to you; it wasn't just performance, it had to do with residue.

At the Clocktower, graphite was arranged in a pattern on the floor. Just before the show opened, an electric organ with no legs was placed on the floor. It was a very beautiful, very pristine installation. Then the German shepherd, which had been kept overnight in a storage room, was dragged through the graphite in a circular manner and placed on the keyboard of the organ. As rigor mortis set in, the position of the dog's body changed radically, and the sound coming out of the organ changed according to the shifting weight of rigor mortis. Because the dog had been dragged through the graphite, the graphite surface became a large drawing. It was a very funereal piece, yet it was joyful, because noise was coming from the dog. The piece accepted death; it treated death with honor.

Mounting a dead dog on an electric organ gave you a slightly sinister reputation. In fact, the dog was not killed for the show, and we had the papers to prove it. When the police arrived, you produced documentation, as you said you would. In no way would you kill a dog for a show. This was important later on, when other artists became involved in Destruction Art—sacrificing objects or animals. To

my knowledge, killing or destroying was not something you were ever involved in. True?

DO In fact, I started using puppets in 1974 because my performances started getting dangerous. The pieces that used my children were becoming more volatile, I started to use surrogates. I refer to this period as "post-performance," a return to installation.

AH Your *return* to installation? To me, you were doing installations all along.

DO I see everything up to 1974 as installations. The perverse act was to take traditional figurative elements and situate them in radical Body Art. It was the double-edged aspect I liked, the discomfort, particularly when I started to dress dolls. I began to think that maybe I'd slipped into the "Twilight Zone."

AH Didn't you make marionettes when you were a boy?

DO I took a marionette class about 1950, when I was twelve, from Clayton Pinkerton at Arts and Crafts College in Oakland. We had to cast the head or make it from papier-mâché and paint it. Then we'd have to deal with the clothes. I think my mother made the outfits.

AH Did you ever become adept at manipulating them?

DO Absolutely. The performance was really what I was into. I'd go around and give marionette shows with my sister at children's hospitals, wherever they wanted us. We did "Beauty and the Beast." Our shows were on a level above the puppets on early television like Howdy Doody and Jerry Mahoney.

AH What about the puppet pieces as surrogates? *Attempt to Raise Hell*, 1974 (pp. 94-95), was particularly shocking for me to see. When I walked into the gallery, I saw this figure, and it was frightening. Funny and frightening.

DO There are at least four configurations culminating from my art. The results vary from creating works that don't make it, to works that function well. *Attempt* was a kind of red herring. I was reeling off a line that was very coherent. I came face to face with certain conditions—in this case, embarrassment. When you think of certain pieces and fantasize what they will be like, what kind of a response they might elicit, you catch yourself facing taboos. Sometimes it's not only difficult for you to pull off the work, it's difficult to make yourself do the work at all.

Attempt was kind of disturbing, in that it came out of nowhere. It's one of the pieces I distrust a bit. Back then, if an idea persisted in my thinking, or if I caught myself drawing or writing the words, "attempt to raise hell," for more than five or six weeks, I would eventually have to make the piece, even though it might be a mistake.

AH Is this because you were reacting against labels?

DO There was a certain discomfort after doing the raw Body Art. Critics said we were moving into another definition of sculpture—sculpture as energy, sculpture as genetics, whatever. Then to come up with this little figure; it was very dangerous. But I was absolutely obsessed with the idea of a bell and a metal head.

AH Dennis, let's leave fatherhood and surrogate parenthood and get back to the subject of evil.

DO Well, I think the artist has to experience some sort of union with evil forces, if not blatantly and consistently, at least to understand the proximity of such forces. Otherwise, his work is one-dimensional. And if you're going to flirt with subversive forms, you have to bring them in to certain degrees if you think you can handle them, because they're there. Otherwise, you find yourself skirting issues because of some preconceived sense of morality, ethics, and fear. If you're a reporter and you have a choice of whom you want as a cell mate, for instance, you would probably pick the most horrendous roommate. If you are psychologically agile and can flirt with danger in the name of art, you should go after it.

Second Generation Image. Iron/Boat., 1988. Wood, fiberglass silkscreened video screen static, mirror. 6' × 8' × 8'.

AH Now we are talking about motivation. Is there another interpretation that has more to do with the physical manifestation of a piece? What is it within a piece that gives the viewer the sense of danger or risk? Take the machines. Most of them suggested the possibility that something was going to be released, that something could fall, or that something was to be shot across the room. There's even the risk that a machine might work. What was the point of entry or re-entry into the unconscious that got you to the danger zone in the factories and machine pieces?

DO When I started making machines, I thought they were a valid development from my early Conceptual Art, which was unstable, dematerialized, and found its appearance through documentation, quite often on video or film. I characterized machines as a passage, not a stasis. They were not couched in permanent material. The development of the *Factories* series was an attempt to continue with the cerebral arena but to engage in a more physical art. So, the machines were considered metaphors for a thought process. That was my entry.

The initial works were considered cerebral architecture. The early piece at P.S. 1, *Way Station Launching an Obsolete Power*, 1979 (pp. 120-21), had elements that seemed to be unstable. There was a conveyor belt that went out the window; the structure was set on a launching ramp. It really wanted to go someplace else. Templates hung from the ceiling, indicating some adjustability—something could enter in. It had slits in the roof, like a chamber in a rifle, where other templates, which had the negative shape of a bullet cut into them, hung. In other words, it had a sufficient number of parallel physical characteristics, so one could build a case that it was trying to assimilate a mental climate—the instability, the impermanence, the shaky attitude of, perhaps, the creative process one was trying to concretize.

Dead Beats, 1988. Steel, perforated steel, fiberglass, silkscreen, fabric, wood, copper. 36″×36″×36″.

Opposite page: Two Objects, 1989. Motor, wood, fabric, timer. 41″×32″×34″.

AH Can we be a little more pedestrian about this particular machine, one I know so well. The machine looked as though it not only could work, but that it *should* work. In fact, parts of it did work. The conveyor belt ran. Viewers were irritated, trying to figure out whether other parts of the piece might work if they were at the museum at a certain time. They even wondered if the piece was turned on. Over the five years it was installed at P.S. 1, I got to watch people watching the piece. As it got older and older, and more and more shabby, things kept falling off. Visitors would say, "Well, one part of it doesn't work, right?" People would go to the main office and ask, "What's going on?" The piece always seemed to the innocent viewer to be politically charged. Perhaps it had something to do with nuclear waste.

DO This kind of sculpture was standing in for mental mechanisms, fractured mechanisms, cerebral structures that are hard to visualize, hard to know about. To ask these machines to somehow physically translate and, perhaps, make visible the things that one is not even sure exist in a cognitive structure is a bit pretentious. Quite often they were criticized because they seemed unnecessarily large. However, works of

this sort could be large, and I felt their size was justified, since they used industrial, architectural elements to set things in motion. They borrowed from the iconography of oil derricks, electrical towers, and other industrial elements.

AH The skeet machine piece, *Scan*, 1979 (p. 119), was a particularly elaborate and threatening machine. You changed a sport like skeet, where marksmen fire at clay discs hurled into the air, into a metaphor for what happens when we send a thought into the world. Where was it done?

DO It was installed at the Kunstverein in Stuttgart in 1979 in a very big room. Behind a shield was a skeet machine that shot skeet through a circle in the middle of the room. There was another shield on the other side of the room that also had a skeet machine. So missiles fired at each other with a potential collision.

AH Dennis, it's a completely ridiculous piece that took up a tremendous amount of space; the viewer didn't get to see very much. It was dangerous, and very loud, requiring constant maintenance. Expensive too, using up hundreds of dollars of clay pigeons. It was one of the stupidest pieces you ever did.

DO No, in a sense it was one of the best. It came from a piece called *Beyond the Tunnel of Hate*, 1979, that was done at Kent State, in a gallery called the Eels Gallery, a suburban open-air space. The piece I did there, a prelude to *Scan*, was only seen by students. It was a covered tunnel about eight feet high that ran eighty feet from the forest and entered the doorway in the gallery. The tunnel was armed in the back with a skeet machine.

It was a covered arcade, an above ground tunnel—a round, arched tunnel with a closed pathway that

Opposite page: Steam Forest with Phantom Limbs, 1988. Cast fiberglass, blown glass, hot plates, electrical timer. 48″ × 40″ × 30″.

Below: Murder in Hawaiian Shirts, 1990. Celastic, silkscreened fabric, plastic toys. 36″ × 60″ × 48″.

led to the gallery's front door. In the first room of the gallery, there was a trough built out of steel that hung from the ceiling on chains. In the next room was a series of sheetrock walls with holes in the shape of missiles. Behind the walls, pointed through the holes, was a very high powered blower fan. Also behind the walls, comprising the last part of the piece, were objects that looked like molds, made out of plywood. They were raw looking and were distributed around the floor, as if you poured cement inside of them and then broke them apart.

The exhibition was the skeet machine firing, almost every second, through this tunnel, into the gallery. As the skeet flew into the space at tremendous speed, they shattered. They'd whistle through the tunnel, whistle through the gallery, hit the launch, and splinter onto the walls. As they whizzed through the walls, the fan would try to blow them away and steer them in another direction. The pieces of skeet slowly collected inside the molds. Over the course of ten days these molds or collectors were slowly filled with the shattered parts of clay discs. The installation was closest to raw thought, a thought going into a chamber—a mind—being formed and finding its way into these molds.

AH Just the name "Kent State" is ominous. It stands for something, for middle America and middle America's children who were protesting the Vietnam War. For you to do this particular piece at Kent State had a lot of overtones. Your work during this time had a lot to do with the energy of projection.

DO These *Factories* came out of a reaction against the idea of virtuosity that is very much the basis of signature art—a body of an artist's work takes the same recognizable form over and over again. I've always been suspicious of virtuosity or dexterity, because I think the artist who is engaged in these solutions often becomes alienated from the deeper impulses that can be brought into the art-making process. An urgency is left out. Another related problem in approaching the art-making process is the problem of entropy. If your beginning point is cerebral, as mine often is, the act of making something physical, is often working toward a slow cooling down. That is, the art object becomes distanced from the mental temperatures that instigated it.

The structural factory was an exteriorized mental facsimile; in the *Factories* series, the fantasy was in building this armature and holding back the raw material (coal, etc.) with rubber straps and aiming it at these central arenas with their adjustable elements (gates, revolving doors, etc.) I was creating an armature, but not firing the idea through it. These *Factories* were like a cerebral catcher's mitt, ready to catch the idea impulse that was always held back. In fact, I called one of these pieces *Waiting Room for the Midnight Special*, 1979 (p. 118).

AH They weren't pretentious works because they weren't over-produced. The viewer didn't get the whole story, but he did get the sense of risk and danger in the work that you and say, Acconci, were doing at the time. Later on, Acconci eliminated risk in his work, you kept pushing the dangerous aspects. You and Acconci were involved in production with extremely destructive possibilities to yourselves and others. You were trying to build primitive machines, like the skeet machine (p. 119) and firework pieces (pp. 133-149).

DO It's interesting how quickly Body Art became confrontational in the hands of American artists. Risk and danger were ingredients in Body Art that just felt right. Unlike method acting, Body Art was real. In being real it participated with the real world, which is dangerous. It was clear and logical to include real danger in that art—not the illusion of danger, or artifice. It made a piece better. You made one work with that commitment and you made one work without it, and it was clear which was better. So danger became an almost formal ingredient.

AH Let's talk about the differences between Body Art going on in America and "ritualistic art" in Europe.

Whirlpool, 1989. Cast fiberglass, water, electric pump, sailboat. 36″ × 30″ × 30″.

DO Well, some art occurring here in a Body/Performance Art context could be discussed in terms of ritual. Some of Acconci's pieces were very ritualistic. Terry Fox took clues from Joseph Beuys in some respects. If you look at it, quite a bit of what was going on in America was concerned with ritual, including some of my work. The gigantic fingerprints, *Identity Stretch*, 1970-75 (pp. 102-03). The diagrams of my father and my daughter, *Polarities*, 1972 (p. 82).

AH But did the Americans and the Europeans have different motives? Take the Austrians, Otto Muelle and Hermann Nitsch and their "blood art."

DO There was a disjuncture. The Americans had a dialogue going on with image. They were looking for a summation of the essentials of a piece in one or two images. They aimed for a coherent graphic depiction, even though that's not at all what the work was about. Much of the ritualistic work going on in Europe was difficult to even subject to documentation. It was truly performance.

AH Maybe we Americans need one-liners, or, unlike the Europeans, didn't want to spend hours watching a bunch of lunatics on their hands and knees dressed in togas. The "blood artists" affected me. In 1967, in Munich, I cleaned up a gallery after one of Hermann Nitsch's performances. The floor was covered with at least three inches of blood. But you could call my dislike for this art, the maid's view of art: How hard is it to move? Can you dust around it? Does it leak?

DO You may have been intimate with this art, but it never really affected the American direction. Being an American, as work became more revolting and disgusting, more shields were dropped, and we were exposed as raving maniacs. We wanted to stop that. In fact, Acconci did some pieces where the audience was able to stop the performance if they wanted to. It was in his script; he would repeat a violent act until an audience member stopped him. In America no one tried to stop him. You could have committed murder on stage in New York City in the 1970s and no one would have stopped you.

AH I remember the 1970s in New York as a time of intense open discussion, and the 1980s as a time of intimate, elegant interchanges. Is this just my age, or did issues about art in New York drastically shift? One of the interesting things about being in Europe in the 1980s was that, unlike New York, people frequently discussed art issues. Düsseldorf, for instance, was at its best in the 1980s. Interesting art came not by chance, but out of the life or death situations that young artists felt and lived. In the 1970s we believed, with almost religious zeal, that a whole movement could die if artists were not willing to articulate why they were doing what they were doing at the time they were doing it. If an artist didn't defend his ideas, the ideas would disappear from criticism, from exhibition.

DO Some artists are strategic and logical about their concerns, and their decisions are partly held in check by critical co-conspirators. In other words, they carefully position their circle of protectors. As they evolve, year after year, their protectors insist on a certain credibility in their work, a protective skin. You find the same kind of behavior among students in secondary schools. There are well-behaved students who are careful about their social behavior, careful about what they produce. They are in unison with a certain social order and they never take dangerous steps. They operate carefully. This is partially true of the practitioners of Conceptual and Minimal Art. It is quite predictable to find individuals who parley their careers in this methodical manner, united as a group.

AH This brings us back to you, Dennis. By persisting in being a wacky experimenter you've dodged a categorical envelope, but you can be accused of being too phlegmatic, too disassociated, of spending your life making work that has resulted in too many categories. You have made eight, nine, or ten different, specific bodies of work. And, perhaps, one could say you didn't follow any of them through, that you didn't care enough, that you didn't make a body of work that you could be responsible

Above the Wall of Electrocution, 1989. Steel rack, cable, animal masks, electric blowers, fabric, electric cord, electric plugs, time delay relay. 48" × 200" × 200".

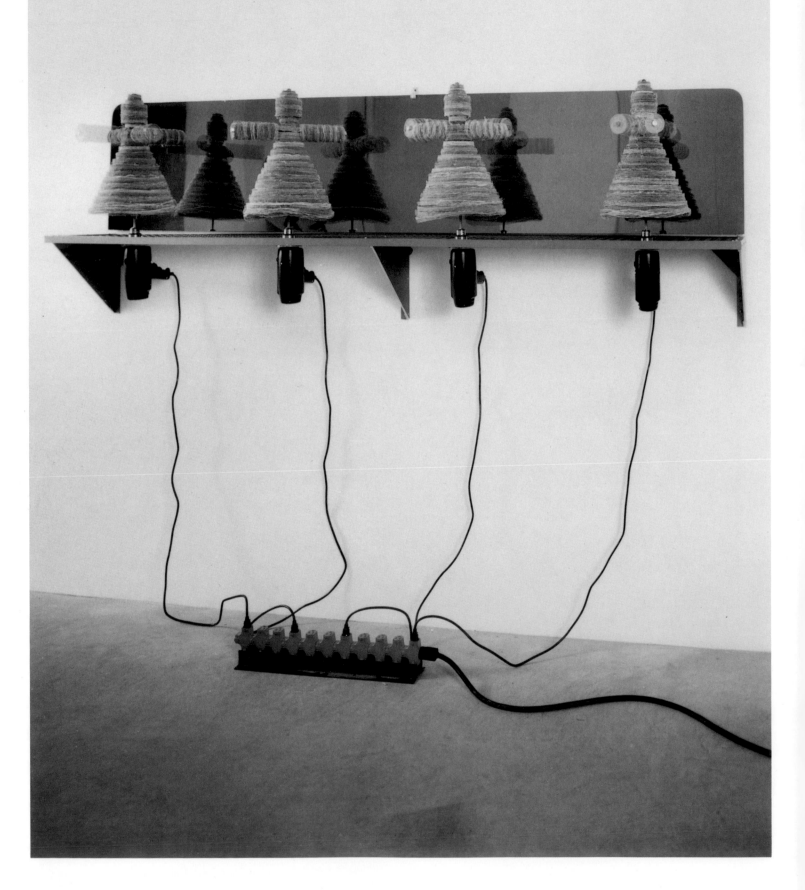

for. One might not be able to look at a work you have made and comfortably say, "That's a Dennis Oppenheim."

DO Some qualities of an artist's work might fall into a signature zone. That is, when you look at a Donald Judd or a Richard Long, there is a signature quality. In advertising it is important to repeat a logo over and over again, so that it achieves a certain density in people's minds. It is important to realize that a signature is a device, a proven device. Most people who are signature artists behave themselves. In our society there is a demand that work continue on a low-level gestalt, where ultimately one body of work blends into another. A certain familiarity makes it easy to fit into museum collections for instance.

It's very easy to tell yourself that such a strategy works. It does work. But strategy has very little to do with the spiritual, creative mechanics of the individual. It has absolutely no relationship to the way cells function or don't function. Strategy is artificial, synthetic. So what constitutes an artist's signature claim on classical works, is often the product of a short-circuited vision. You need to find rigorous, alternate avenues in the creative process. I've tested the sort of mindset I would need to perpetuate signature art. I can't do it. I could never defend, nor could I even engage such a diabolically strategic course of making my work appear connected. It's antithetical to the creative process.

AH Then is the signature of your work its diversity?

DO In many ways one of the elements found in looking at work after work as it unfolds is the secret dialogue that takes place with the power structure, with elitist signature art. There are works being done as buttresses, as methods of escape and attack. My work is partly guided and directed through a diabolical conversation with the mainstream, because there's no way you can co-exist with the mainstream as a disenfranchised agitator. You are caught up in it as an underground underdog. You can't simply be on the defensive, exhausting your work on targets directed at the art world. Your work has to be digested through a critical format that you're indebted to, that you're always engaged in.

AH Is what you are calling signature art antithetical to the creative process, or is it antithetical to *your* creative process?

Opposite page: Four Spinning Dancers. (From the Power Tool Series)., 1989. Anodized aluminum, mirror, electric drills, buffing discs, electric plugs, steel, timer. 48″ × 60″ × 24″. *Below, left: Badly Tuned Cow,* 1989.

Fiberglass, wax, steel, silkscreened wood, black lights. 72″ × 96″ × 96″. *Below, right: Second Generation Image,* 1989. Fiberglass, wax, wood, papier-mâché. 54″ × 18″ × 43″.

Image Dissonance. (Coffee Cup)., 1989. Wire
armature, foam, steel plate. 48″ × 200″ × 200″.

DO I am psychologically unable to participate in a signature art career campaign. However, there are individuals who do this quite well, but I'm suspicious about the kind of career evolution in which the strategy is so conscious, perpetrated with such accuracy, so studiously controlled.

How can an artist have a parallel dialogue with himself, as he is evolving? God knows that artists, quite often more than other people, are thrown into volatile storms as they evolve. This has always been what I thought art's content was—a way of feeding this experience into a form. While you're being tossed about in an evolutionary storm on the one hand, and you're holding on to your signature style with the other, there is a great disparity between the information you are going to pass from one hand to the other. Many artists separate art and life to protect the rarity and purity of their work.

AH You're a guy who's always changing his handwriting. Let's talk about when you started drawing in the air. When did you do the first firework piece?

DO Well, the piece at the Kunsthaus in Zurich, *Second Sight for a Staircase*, in 1981 (p. 133), did not originally include fireworks. Then I changed it, unbeknownst to the organizers. I turned it into my first piece in the *Fireworks* series. There was a swinging pendulum that had a butane tank attached to it, which swung closely to a catherine wheel made with rockets.

AH Did the curators and the director know that the piece was going to function in the middle of their collection of Van Goghs?

Below: Black Pool, 1990. Wood, steel, aluminum rods, billiard balls, bowling balls, black pipe, felt. 73″ × 97″ × 48″.

Opposite page: Virus (detail), 1989. Cast plaster, aluminum rod, scientific clamps. 72″ × 72″ × 72″.

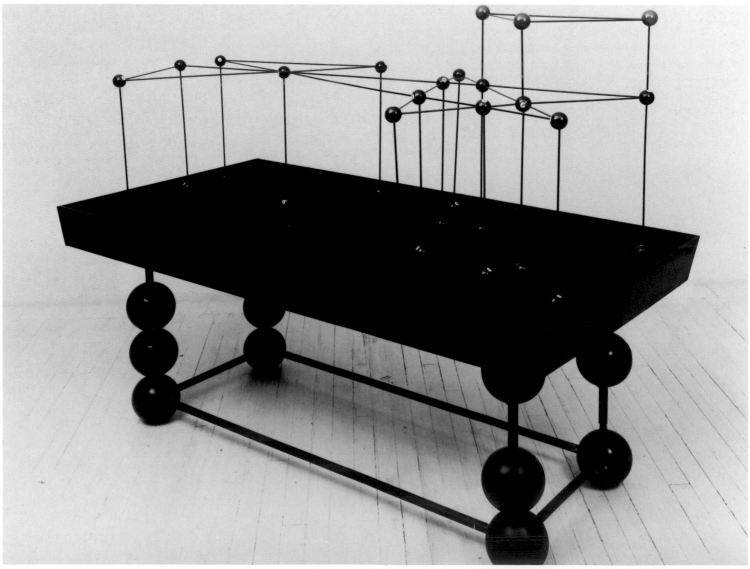

DO I was buying fireworks. Everyone was quite concerned about the artwork, as was I, but I suggested we give it a try. Finally, it was successful. It created an edge during the opening.

AH An edge of tension? Was there any fallout of the smoke on the Van Goghs?

DO Not really. Everything was controlled. But there is a chronology of the *Fireworks* series. The next piece was conceived as a group of elements that all had a relationship. It was originally titled *An Armature for Projection and Exorcism*, 1981-82 (pp. 134-35), and installed at the Bonlow Gallery in New York. Exorcism meant the appearance of secret bodies within the structure itself. Actually, a system of ghosts was to emanate from a labyrinth. But as soon as the first fuse was lit, it became apparent to everyone that they were in danger. One firework lit another, and then lit ten. A chain reaction set in. The idea of escalation, as related to quantum mechanics, physics, was important to this work, as well as the idea of being out of control. Everything was in a state of chaos, uncontrollable release, and pictorial imaging. Within a minute the smoke was extremely thick and greasy.

AH No one actually got hurt, did they?

DO No. The life-threatening aspect was not at all interesting to me; it was never my subject. As far as the functioning of the "exorcism," it behaved perfectly. It was exactly what I had hoped for. The suggestion that this armature was truly lifting off its cold steel frame was the effect I was after. And as it became airborne, it approached the sanction of the concept; it became what I had imagined—thoughts emanating from the artist who had thought the piece through. It approached its origin, its mental genesis. The piece realized everything I had theorized. Unfortunately, none of this could be communicated, what with the horrendous overtone of danger.

I have difficulty conjuring up the excitement that was experienced ten years ago in regards to my machines. I'm suspicious, a little cool on these pieces. I remember the excitement I felt when I started them and know it was legitimate. Then the machines got contaminated; there was a lot of extraneous dialogue. I was pulled in various directions, ultimately off course. This sounds natural and good, but I, who started out with an incredible view about how a metaphor and structure could be coupled together, ended up feeling like the walking wounded, surrounded by rockets flying through the air—a real battlefield. The ten years given over to the machines could be as substantial as the Earth Art, but I'm just not sure.

AH How important to you is the idea of instability in general, and to your art in particular?

DO I've been agreeable to internal and external weather conditions entering my work from the beginning. A period of operation on unstable ground is something I'm very familiar with. The act of making art for me is as if you are falling. The ground moves away, and you hold your breath and fall. The mind separates to catch you. It catches you by suspending an idea like a parachute. My overwhelming sensation in entering work has always been a rapid heart beat. I shake, then a tremor begins. By then I know I'm falling, and I begin to throw out images as if one can suspend me, carry me away. You want to throw out the images that can save your life. Thoughts are constantly pressured into visual images at this high altitude—language, words are sputtered out, quickly changing into image structures. You need a coherent image structure before you hit the ground, otherwise you go right through and keep falling. I like to work on fast-moving trains or in crowded bars. I always carry a pad of paper with me to catch myself in those places that have a high level of commotion.

AH At the time you were working with the *Fireworks* series, did you believe you were, as an artist, our surrogate, trying to invent armature to battle with the forces of chaos and fear? Were you going into the dark regions of your own imagination to set up theatrically sculptural situations?

Slow Clap for Satie, 1989. Acrylic, wood, steel, motors, ficus trees, pots, turntables, vacuum formed masks, tape player, loop recording of an Erik Satie piano piece, timer. 120″ × 250″ × 250″.

DO I don't seem to go into regions as much as I'm pulled into them or fall into them. Clearly the *Factories* were getting progressively more charged from 1979 to 1983. As counterparts to my thought process, they moved closer and closer to so-called dark regions. The mental landscape became craggy and sharp, with traps, cliffs, and ravines. Works like *Final Stroke*, 1980 (pp. 130-31), and *Accelerator for Evil Thoughts*, 1983 (p. 144), were made then. Pieces had constant indications of impasse, like tracks moving on a collision course. Elements on pulleys and counterweights indicated adjustability or behavior, but more often entrapment. Mental overload, trauma, hysteria.

AH These pieces were very complicated. On one level there was the immediate potential of an event that was loaded. On the other hand, there was another level of time, the future potential, which meant the explosion. On a third level, there was the past, the smoke, the people standing around, the memory of what just happened. So a wider notion of sculpture became possible that included these three levels of time. Were you consciously reacting to the art you were seeing at the time or did you have a desire to rewrite art history?

DO A lot of what drives me is based on early suppositions I made, suppositions that have been made by other artists as well. Call it a certain kind of dissatisfaction gained from looking at a lot of art. So much work is based on the simple process of being dissatisfied and having unresolved feelings about what you see. You end up trying to fill in where you feel there are missing links, building your work out of an urge to put yourself into theoretical requirements you find missing, engaging in an academic process of constructing your work.

AH There's that word, "urge," which could be called the search for authenticity. Authenticity of artistic exploration. Authenticity of work. Authenticity of the residue. In each body of work we've talked about, there has been the impetus, the urge to capture the dark nights, the bad times—the good times too, but there is more of an urge to explore the darkness. At the same time, you are careful to stop short of coming up with anything you could call a position. No matter what happens to you, you continue to push things, resisting manufactured positions.

DO Some conditions that surround artists are unavoidable. There's very little that they can do about certain philosophical, psychological, or theoretical stances they take. You have to maneuver against your will, against your natural inclinations. I'm used to such maneuvers. If Body Art did anything, it gave me a chance of living with a very high level of discomfort in art-making. I'm not suggesting that painters are not suffering by engaging their work, but Body Art was a real exercise in endurance, and it put me close to behavioral zones that were extremely uncomfortable to assume simply to do the work.

AH Tell me about endings. What about the firework piece that led to the end of the series?

DO *Launching Structure #3*, 1982, looked like Cape Canaveral. In that work I was seduced by the fireworks themselves. I realized I had created a sculpture that was moving dangerously into the clutches of Constructivist iconography. Somehow it got out of hand. I felt alienated, and when I looked at the work I was like a kid standing next to a Saturn rocket. In my urge to make my own mental anatomy appear through my sculptures, I lost myself in the actual armature. I didn't feel I could continue making something I was so estranged from.

AH Estrangement seemed to fuel a lot of other artists in the 1980s. Do you think this sense of alienation changed the art world a lot? In terms of what was supported? What could be made? What options were open to artists? What risks could they take?

DO A funny kind of paradox existed. Art seemed to be going forward by going backward in the 1980s. You had a movement where artists took on Neo-Expressionism by referring to the early twentieth century. And post-Modernism came on the scene. Clearly the 1980s encouraged a schizophrenic

Figure Skating, 1990. Wood, copper, acid-treated aluminum. 11″ × 200″ × 45″.

Digestion: Gypsum Gypsies, 1989. Papier-
mâché, wax, cast resin, copper tube, gas line,
gas tanks. 60″ × 180″ × 120″.

dialogue that added layers. Art wasn't moving in a linear direction as much as it was oscillating.

AH Did that schizophrenia interest you?

DO I liked the perversity of art moving forward by going backward. I liked appropriation and commodity based work, even though I felt alienated from the discourse that was extrapolating from second generation Conceptualism. People were looking at Joseph Kosuth's work as art that was unable to communicate to a large art audience. Neo-Expressionism was partly a reaction against Conceptualism, and the fact that it seemed so vapid it fed into the commodity-based discourse, which was reactionary. The 1980s were filled with three year slots of reactionary movements.

AH Well, the eighties did play themselves and us out. That's why we're in good shape now; the 1990s are a reflection of the 1970s. Many of us who were involved in radical adventures are seen to be people who hold integrity in the palm of our hands. The 1980s pushed commercialism so far that a large percentage of people who had become involved with art—who planned their lives and found themselves with some very different goals—are now gagging. I'm not suggesting it is a rejection of money that has caused this to change in the 1990s; it is the inability of anyone to get money anymore— a fact that has turned the art community into thinking about what is important or should be important. So, people have become more interested in Earth and Body Art and in early non-saleable museum-based activities. Which leads me to ask you about money. What is your relationship to money as a person who has made work for twenty-five years that is not easily collected?

DO Well, it's quite true that in 1968, operating within the Earth Art context, there was very little expectation of financial stability. As Body Art followed, dematerializing the object even more, this expectation was further reduced. In fact, it was then that the notion of selling disappeared. I used to lecture for a living. The work that followed did not meet with much commercial success and, of course, the *Factories* were never sold. It is true that I retain most of this work; some was given to museums. Obviously I have thought about this, and on many occasions I've received tremendous support; although no one would buy a machine piece, they would consider a drawing. Earth Art was collected through documentation.

The market somehow pulls you into its wake when you least expect it, particularly when you're concentrating on what you're doing. There is an impact of success that for some artists can be damaging. We all know problems arise often when the market looms, entangling the artist, clouding his or her vision, changing impulses. However, I don't think I've experienced that yet.

AH When you say not commercial, what do you mean? Not easily sold?

DO Not sold. When I have exhibitions and nothing sells, it doesn't phase me. It's not as if I'm jaded or so shell-shocked, I can't speak. It simply doesn't matter. In the 1970s, when we had shows where nothing would sell, we'd just throw things away.

AH But in twenty-five years, I've never heard you complain about being broke; you've somehow kept a balance, making work which interests you and living reasonably well. How do you do it? Alchemy?

DO I've been able to stabilize my drawings to a certain tempo and radicalize my sculpture regardless of any momentary calm I might hit with the commercial market.

AH While we're thinking about your drawings and how they relate to your sculpture, let's take a step back. Let me try to establish the lineage of a piece of sculpture in relation to a drawing, and you tell me if I've got the sequence right, how one relates to the other.

First, there's the nightmare that comes to you. It can be during the day or at night. It comes from problems, conscious or unconscious. Then, there's your attempt to think through the image of the nightmare. Then, you think out the image. Next comes what I call the "napkin drawing," which is not the "drawing" drawing, it's a description drawing. You develop aspects of a piece carefully in a napkin drawing; other diagrams describe the general shape. Then, comes the meeting, where, on a number of napkins, you describe what you want to your collaborators. Then, after the meeting and several discussions with your collaborators, you make specific engineering drawings that are produced by collaborators and corrected by you. Things change. Then, there are more meetings. "This will not work, Dennis. What do you want to happen?"

The engineering drawings are refined and fabrication begins. Elements are fabricated either separately or jointly in one place, or in several places. They are assembled at the production site. At this point things go wrong and changes are made again, either because things haven't been described correctly, or because they don't work. Changes are made still another time, either by you or the fabricator/collaborators, until the piece is resolved. It happens over many sleepless nights. Finally the doors open; the public comes in. After the opening, the piece rests for a while, and you express your dissatisfaction, returning with the collaborators to make more changes. Near the end, probably right after the public presentation, the drawings happen.

DO That's a fantastic interpretation! It refers mostly to the *Factories* projects. However, before that body of work I had no assistance. I was like everyone else moping around Canal Street, looking for materials, props I could afford, trying my best to develop menial skills to make sure things didn't fall apart. Constantly going to shops, stuffing my car and losing half the contents on the way to the gallery. Electrocuting myself, blowing fuses, standing in the dark corner of the gallery during the opening in complete shock, realizing as the motors were heating up, circuits were collapsing; trains were colliding too soon.

I wanted to be a painter: put up the work, enjoy the opening, have a good night's sleep. My shows haunted me from beginning to end. Calls from the gallery flooded in. "Come over and repair the exhausted elements." I would run down West Broadway and up the stairs, only to enter a room of frozen elements, the smell of burnt electrical motors filling the air. A few bewildered spectators would be scratching their heads; the dealer was tapping her foot.

AH It must have been exhausting. You were doing a major piece every month. No wonder you retired for a time after the *Fireworks* series.

DO You know, twenty-five years is a long time. Changes are bound to occur. The artist is not necessarily an endless fountain, spurting out work in a constant rhythm. Art happens to me in a multitude of ways, and believe me, at times it seems to abandon you, leaving not a trace. Or more likely, you empty yourself of it. One simply can't keep firing themselves up. This is as it should be, and I can't imagine any other way. I use the expression "running in place" a lot to describe a condition in which the artist is moving but going nowhere. I recognize this in myself and can even pull aside works I've made while engaged in this mental state. I'm quite hard on the works I do that come from this kind of masturbation. But I show them sometimes, because I know that in their inability to take off, they are nevertheless building up steam. I operate in what you could call a high crisis level; it's a momentum, a swing. As I'm building up, I know the price I will have to pay. I will always go back down.

AH Let's talk about your recent work. It looks very different from anything you've done. The big lips that recall Marilyn Monroe? Hawaiian shirts? Popular culture? Why now? If your early work was a dialogue with Minimalism, is your recent work meant to respond to post-Modernism?

DO As you know, it is just as dangerous to shield yourself from influences as it is to be consumed by them. One has to differentiate between the electrical connections that occur while reading, say, Beckett or Joyce—how such ideas can and do bleed into your work, and how self-conscious, indulgent, and sheer plagiarism of forces with absolutely no personal resonance feels. Dialogues are held on many levels. Some are deep utterances, minds speaking to minds on sub-levels; each

Combined Expressions, 1990. Galvanized
steel. 120″ × 120″ × 120″.

Kissing Racks, 1990. Bottle racks, colored
cast resin, cord, electric turntables.
48″ × 40″ × 34″.

occupying the other's mental field, moving in unison through an archetypal landscape. Exterior energy, or feedback, is best ricocheted within your own system, echoing against your mythic heroes. As long as what comes in has to prove its durability and congruency by co-existing with the anatomy you already have, it's okay.

In forcibly rejecting an incoming thought-construct, one is already being controlled by it, and it continues in waves of self-conscious rejection until it surreptitiously affects the deep skin of your ideas. Better to let these things rush in, see if they can cling to your bones, it's the way you grow. My new work is simply breathing in different air; some of it is fresh. Obviously these new pieces are ricocheting off my mental bones, occasionally discovering something I am unaware of. When I shake, so does the work, and in doing so hopefully recognize what I'm looking at and how looking at it is affecting me.

AH One of the threads in post-Modernism is the element of nostalgia. Another thread that runs through the work is a fascination with consumer culture.

DO I'm too old to engage in the commodity discourse. I must admit I'm not the least bit interested in it. What goes through all of the work—from the machine pieces on—is the notion of a breaking point. Piece after piece is about trying to push through a sort of envelope or membrane. If you look at the transfer drawings with my children (pp. 72-73), they are about passing information through a child to get to a time zone I can't get to because of my age. There's an attempt to fracture the membrane. My new work is no different. It simply operates within a new image bank, an extended vocabulary. My position now is at the end of the pendulum. What I am trying to do is build up another system of momentum that will release another swing.

AH I happen to think the recent work is a breakthrough. The spirit pieces, *Above the Wall of Electrocution*, 1989 (p. 165) are beautiful. The deer, *Digestion: Gypsum Gypsies*, 1989 (pp. 176-77), are startling. The lips, *Kissing Racks*, 1990 (pp. 181 and 184-85), is one of the ugliest, most repulsive pieces I've seen. However, the recent work looks slick, like it's borrowing from advertising and Pop Art.

DO When I left for Korea in 1988, I had reams of notes about objects in physiological states. I was trying to find an image match, a condition of external objects that paralleled my own physiological condition, which I felt was unstable. So, the oblique conversation with commodity-based work, deconstruction, and simulacra was peripheral. But I'm not sure how able I am to pin down the impulses that led to those things because my mind was so tuned to the physiological, the genetic. I've been using words like "diagnostics" and "mercy killing," in my recent work. *Badly Tuned Cow*, 1989 (p. 167), is another genetic work. So is *Digestion* with the gas going through the deer's antlers.

AH The recent work leaves you open for serious attack.

DO All right, I like attacks. I'm used to them.

Could I move this conversation into what I still feel to be the most mysterious area of all, that of form, or more specifically, inspired form. When I talk about aerial acrobatics, falling, suspension, tremor, fracturing the envelope, swinging, it's simply a desperate attempt to describe the edges of form. Content is easy, even inspired content. But form, that's another animal. I guess when you fall, you move your arms a certain way, trying to save yourself; you're grabbing at air. Well, you just put a mind out there, in front of you, and you shape it out of the desperation. You blow oxygen in its face, and you get a reading. It's all through the air; you notice it. You're breathing in form, and you can tell because things are attaching themselves, going one way and not the other. There's always a shortness of breath; you're panting, as if you're breathing around a box. It's form! Despite yourself, form is the blanket you catch yourself in. Inspired form is pulled out of the atmosphere and made thick by your need to survive. As I'm saying this, it sounds pretentious and Formalist, but I'm really talking about urgency, the need for urgency survives in all art movements. I even detect some urgency in Jeff Koons's desire to wed Cicolina.

AH When you talk about the new work, you keep using the words "tremor," "agitation," "shaky." Why?

DO Everything—the drums, the toasters, the spirits, the airplanes—everything is colliding, dissipating, falling apart. There's a kind of image jitters which refers to video overload. There's a feeling of sensory overload on the part of the artist, myself. There's no approach to an object that isn't shaky. Those are conditions that lie beyond a discourse on post-modern postures.

AH The new work seems to have more of an emphasis on color. And there's a craft element. The objects are both beautiful and ugly. Beautifully ugly, and so well crafted that they're extraordinarily physical.

DO Well, you know I was never against craft, even though it's so easy for me to be sloppy. But crafted objects are another suspicious area. They show a certain kind of insecurity, because the artist is giving so much attention to the finish, that he or she is afraid there are no guts.

AH The work looks pretty obsessive; that giant cowboy boot *Toe to Heel*, 1990 (pp. 184-85), with the ballerina inside is an example of fanatical fashion.

DO It is a fetish. If you're in possession of an idea, quite often you have a relaxed feeling about its execution. If you're unsure of the idea, you tend to make a fetish out of the object, because you get enraptured by the craft. It's a funny situation. The best way to feel is really to be enraptured by the idea; then the craft is less important.

AH When you talk about your work now, you use words that refer to an unstable condition. Why?

DO There is a way of looking at the fireworks as being silly, overdramatic, sentimental, artificial pomp, with no real substance, some of which is true. But I used fireworks because, unlike a pencil line, the trajectories caused by fast-moving sparks are behavioral. They interact with one another, perhaps even collide, very much like my mind does when it is approaching something. The other thing about fireworks are the maps they scribe out. These are urgent schematics; not deliberated or postured by intellectual intervention. The intellect can be a dangerous bedfellow to inspired cause and effects transactions.

It is intellect that bends the mental trajectories too soon, or not soon enough. Fireworks, like thoughts, carry their own intelligence if you let them; not that you shouldn't intervene, but feelings work best here, in the sky. It's feelings that steer impulses; intellect simply weighs too much. Words like tremor, agitation, and so on, are often undernourished descriptions of things I can't really translate.

AH Very little of the conversation we're having is at the level carried on by the so-called Neo Geo artists or the picture theorists who deal with contextual problems; their discussions are far more sophisticated. Bloodless is one word that comes to mind.

DO My work never got enraptured by that, although it flowed through the same rivers. If a philosophical base is legitimately interesting, you test it against the things you feel. Simulation theory. Is it interesting? Derrida? Are you going to throw him away?

AH Is that philosophic base intellectually interesting to you?

DO Frankly, I would like to have a more coherent understanding of deconstruction.

AH You and everybody else.

DO I think it's dangerous to be inflexible at any point to influence. If you are not open to influence, it keeps you at a stasis. I don't like to be challenged because things are difficult enough. But, in a perverse way, I do. And, I like things threatening to my position.

Installation at *Casino Fantasma,* Casino of
the City of Venice, Venice.: *Spirit Notes,* 1990.
Painted trumpets, electric blowers, timers,
fabric, masks. 4″ × 144″ × 96″; *Toe to Heel.
Woman Trapped in a Man's Body.,* 1990.
Aluminum, stitched netting, figure, wax,
electric turntable. 144″ × 96″ × 48″; and
Kissing Racks. 1990. Aluminum, vacuum
formed plastic, cord, electric turntables.
108″ × 96″ × 48″.

CHRONOLOGY

1938
Born September 6, to David A. Oppenheim and Katherine Belknap in Electric City, Washington (formerly named Mason City), where his father is an engineer on Grand Coulee Dam.

1953
Qualifies as Marksman-First Class in the Junior National Rifle Association.

1954
Joins a hot rod club called the Richmond Trojans.

1955
Meets Walter De Maria, a fellow high-school student.
Graduates from Richmond High, Richmond, California.

1958
Marries Karen Cackett, a fellow student at the California College of Arts and Crafts in Oakland, California, where he is a full-time student.

1959
Moves to Honolulu. Attends art classes at the University of Hawaii, Honolulu.
Opens a public relations firm, Oppenheim Associates.
Daughter, Kristin, is born.

1960
Jean Tinguely's "Homage to New York" self-destructs in the sculpture garden at the Museum of Modern Art, New York.

1961
Returns to the San Francisco Bay Area.

1962
Son, Erik, is born.

1964
Teaches at the California College of Arts and Crafts, Oakland.

1965
Receives Bachelor of Fine Arts degree from the California College of Arts and Crafts, Oakland.

1966
Receives a Newhouse Foundation grant to study at Stanford University, Stanford.
Receives a Purchase Award for the painting, *Untitled #2,* included in the exhibition "Max. 24/66" at Purdue University, Lafayette, Indiana. James Rosenquist is a juror.
Moves to New York. Teaches nursery school in Northport, Long Island.

Frequents Mickey Ruskin's bar/restaurant, "Max's Kansas City," with Frosty Meyers, Larry Bell, Michael Steiner, Neil Williams, John Chamberlain, Ronnie Landfield, and David Novoros.

1967
Participates with performance piece in "Plastics West Coast," an exhibition of twenty-two West Coast artists, including John McCracken, Ron Cooper, Charles Ross, and Dewain Valentine.
Sol Lewitt's "Paragraphs on Conceptual Art" appears in the summer issue of *Artforum,* and the term "Conceptual Art" becomes part of the art vocabulary.
Meets and becomes friends with Robert Smithson.
Teaches art at Smithtown Junior High School in Long Island.
Executes the first earthwork, *Oakland Wedge,* in Oakland.
Meets Phyllis Jalbert, a French teacher who is to become his second wife, later in the year.

1968
Travels between California and New York.
Shows scale models and plans for earthworks in "Funk Trucks, etc." at Green Gallery, San Francisco.
First one-person exhibition in New York, at John Gibson Gallery.
Is interviewed by *Newsweek* for an article "The New Art," in which Lucy Lippard coins the phrase, "dematerialization."
Teaches graduate seminars in sculpture at Yale University in New Haven, Connecticut.
Participates with Robert Morris, Michael Heizer, and Robert Smithson in "Earthworks," an exhibition at Dwan Gallery, New York.
Executes a series of snow projects in northern Maine near the Canadian border, including *Annual Rings, Time Pocket,* and *One Hour Run.*
Participates in recorded discussion sessions during December 1968 and January 1969 with Michael Heizer and Robert Smithson in New York.
Second daughter, Chandra, born.

1969
First exhibition in Paris at the Galerie Yvon Lambert.
Meets and becomes friends with Vito Acconci.

Executes earthwork *Directed Seeding/Canceled Crop* at Albert Waalken's farm in Finsterwolde, Holland.
Makes first film, *Backtrack,* with Bob Fiore in New York.
Germano Celant's book, *Art Povera,* is published.
Exhibits photographic documentation of Earth Art in the exhibition, "When Attitudes Become Form," at the Kunsthalle Bern.
Jean-Louis Bourgeois writes and publishes the first major article on Dennis for *Artforum.*
Publishes notebooks, "Catalyst 1967-1970," in *ArtsCanada.*
Meets Gordon Matta-Clark, who assists him on two projects for the exhibition "Earth Art," held at Andrew Dickson White Museum of Art, Cornell University, Ithaca, New York.
Holly Solomon opens 98 Greene Street, an alternative space.

1970
Attends Symposium on Earth Art at the White Museum, Cornell University, with Robert Smithson, Neil Jenney, Gunther Uecker, Hans Haacke, and Richard Long.
Ground Level (Push-ups on Mud), a slide presentation with sound, included in the "Information" exhibition at the Museum of Modern Art, New York.
Frequents *Levine's Restaurant,* operated by Les Levine and Mickey Ruskin.
Becomes summer artist-in-residence at the Aspen Center for Contemporary Art, Colorado, where he makes the films and tapes later compiled as "Aspen Projects."
Jeffrey Lew opens 112 Greene Street, "a socialist art system."
Collaborates with Vito Acconci and Kathy Dillon on the performance piece, "Kiss Transference Project," at the School of the Art Institute of Chicago.

1971
Travels to Argentina for the "Art Systems" exhibition at the Modern Art Museum of Buenos Aires, the first important show of his films and tapes.
Returns to Aspen as summer artist-in-residence. Meets Bruce Nauman, who is also an artist-in-residence.
The Guggenheim Museum cancels Hans Haacke's exhibition about real estate ownership in New York.
Vito Acconci's performance, "Seedbed," takes place at Sonnabend Gallery.

David A. Oppenheim, Dennis's father, dies in Oakland.

1972

Ursula Meyer's book, *Conceptual Art,* is published.

Executes *Polarities, 2000' Shadow Projection,* and the film, *Stewing Around,* with funds received from the John Simon Guggenheim Memorial Foundation Fellowship.

Teaches a graduate seminar in sculpture at the School of the Art Institute of Chicago.

Travels to an international performance festival in Pamplona, Spain, where Phillip Glass and Steve Reich perform.

1973

Produces at Landfall Press in Chicago, "Projects" portfolio, a suite of ten photo-lithographs that document works from 1968-72.

Writes monologue for *Wishing Well,* his first installation using an extended audio track.

Separates from Phyllis Jalbert.

Begins to plan for an exhibition at the Stedelijk Museum with Gijs van Tuyl, curator

Hires a pilot and an aerial photographer to execute and document a sky piece, *Whirlpool—Eye of the Storm,* over El Mirage Dry Lake in California.

Robert Smithson, his pilot, and a photographer are killed in an airplane crash on a rocky hillside nearby the site of the earthwork, *Amarillo Ramp.*

1974

Writes lyrics and records song for the first "surrogate" piece, *Theme for a Major Hit,* in New York, with Roger Welch (drums), Bill Beckley (guitar/vocal), Diego Cortez (electric organ), and Connie Beckley (vocal).

Lectures extensively throughout the United States.

Spends time with Liza Bear, Willoughby Sharp, and Terry Fox at *Avalanche* magazine.

Makes an artist's book, *Indentations,* in cooperation with Galerie Yaki Kornblit in Amsterdam.

Joseph Beuys's *I Like America and America Likes Me,* takes place in New York.

Receives a National Endowment for the Arts Fellowship.

1975

Produces a book and a limited print edition, *Proposals 1967-1974,* published by Lebeer Hossman Editeurs, Brussels,

including sixty-two scaled blueprints of realized projects and proposals.

Participates in two exhibitions organized by the Museum of Contemporary Art in Chicago, "Bodyworks," the first comprehensive American survey of the subject, and "Menace," which focuses on artistic manifestations of threat or dread.

Works with Synapse in Syracuse, New York to produce color video tapes, including *Spinning Knife, Pulling, Like Swatting Flies,* and *Spinning a Yarn.*

Has eleven one-person exhibitions during the year; this number is matched in 1977, and surpassed in 1982 and 1984 with twelve exhibitions. In 1979 he has thirteen one-person exhibitions.

Participates in the summer program at Artpark, Lewiston, New York, with *Identity Stretch.* Also in the program are friends and colleagues Dale Chihuly, Forrest Myers, Alan Saret, Paul Sharits, and Charles Simonds.

1976

First retrospective exhibition at the Museum Boymans van Beuningen, Rotterdam, organized by Johannes van der Wolk.

Shows *Lecture #1* at Framartstudio, Naples, a surrogate piece that incorporates an audiotape that reflects on the death of Robert Smithson and forecasts events that will occur to eleven other artists between 1973-80.

The Institute for Art and Urban Resources opens Project Studio 1 (P.S. 1) in Long Island City. First exhibition, "Rooms," includes Oppenheim's *Broken Record Blues.*

1977

Executes five works on the landscape, including *Wishing The Mountains Madness,* and *Three Downward Blows (Knuckle Marks),* in Lolo, Montana and *Cobalt Vectors—An Invasion,* at the El Mirage Dry Lake, southern California.

Travels to Kassel, Germany, to participate in Documenta 6.

At the inaugural exhibition of the Teheran Museum of Contemporary Art, he presents scale model proposals for outdoor works to be built in the desert using the military as the construction crew.

The New Museum of Contemporary Art opens in New York to show exclusively art created within the past ten years. First show, "Early Work by Five Con-

temporary Artists," includes ten *Sitemarkers,* 1967.

Multiples, Inc., New York, produces "Mind Twist: A Portfolio of Burnt-out Thoughts," a limited edition of ten photographic works from early 1970s that used flares, language, and the landscape.

Publishes notebooks from 1970 to 1974 in Alan Sondheim's book, *Individuals.*

Vito Acconci completes *Red Tapes.*

1978

Ten-year retrospective, organized by Alain Parent, opens at Musée d'Art Contemporain in Montreal and travels to three museums across Canada.

Close friend and colleague, Gordon Matta-Clark dies of cancer at age thirty-five in New York.

Plans for an exhibition to take place the following year with Dr. Jean-Christophe Ammann, Director of the Kunsthalle Basel, Switzerland.

1979

Travels to Basel for exhibition at the Kunsthalle, which moves within the year to the Kunstverein in Stuttgart and ARC 2, Musée d'Art Moderne de la Ville de Paris. At each venue new works are constructed.

Travels with his son Erik to the Midwest, Pacific Northwest, and Canada.

Participates in the Earthworks Symposium about art as land reclamation, sponsored by the King County Arts Commission, Seattle.

The two-person show "Dialogue" with Robert Smithson and Dennis Oppenheim, organized by John Coplans, opens at the Akron Art Institute, Akron, Ohio.

Builds *Power Passage (for Indianapolis)* with students at the Herron School of Art in Indianapolis.

Participates in the exhibition, "Sound," at The Institute for Art and Urban Resources, P.S. 1, with the installation *Way Station Launching An Obsolete Power. (A Thought Collision Factory in Pursuit of Journey). (A Clip in a Rifle Weapon).,* constructed by John Taguiri and Robert Price, fabricators from 1979-81.

Has frequent discussions with the English art critic, Stuart Morgan.

Chandra, eleven, performs with a band in New York nightclubs and releases an album.

Works with Luigi Kurmann, a Swiss technical advisor, who is the main fabricator for sculpture made in Europe from 1979-1982.

1980
Becomes friends with Terry Allen, while both are visiting artists at the Cranbrook Academy of Art in Bloomfield Hills, Michigan.

Meets Jean Tinguely while they work on outdoor sculptures at Wenkenpark in Basel.

Builds the first piece that incorporates fireworks, *Second Sight for a Staircase,* in Geneva.

Visits frequently with John Coplans, who moves to New York.

1981
Builds the monumental installation *Launching Structure #1. An Armature For Projection. (From the Fireworks Series).* for the exhibition, "Metaphor," at the Hirshhorn Museum and Sculpture Garden, Washington, D.C.

1982
The Rijksmuseum Kroller-Muller in Otterlo, Holland, installs *Station For Detaining and Blinding Radio-active Horses,* 1980-82, as a permanent work in the museum sculpture garden.

Marries Alice Aycock, sculptor, in New York City.

Travels to Pistoia, Italy, at the invitation of Guiliano Gori, to participate in a group symposium on art and art institutions, and to create a work, *Formula Compound. A Combustion Chamber. An Exorcism. (From the Fireworks Series).,* on site. Participating international sculptors include the American sculptors, Alice Aycock, George Trakas, and Robert Morris.

Members of the press attend the only full activation of *Launching Structure #2. An Armature for Projection. (From the Fireworks Series).,* at the Bonlow Gallery in Soho. Steven Reichard handles the public relations for the event.

1983
Travels to Tokyo for an exhibition at the Akira Ikeda Gallery.

Separates from his wife, Alice Aycock.

Spends summer in Banff, Canada, producing twenty-nine models and small sculptures from *the Tremor Series,* with assistance of students from the Banff Center.

1984
Makes several trips to Anchorage while the outdoor sculpture, *Image Intervention* is under construction.

Returns to Artpark in Lewiston, New York, for the "ignition" of *Newton Dis-*

covering Gravity, the last piece from the *Fireworks* series.

Travels to Thessaloniki, Greece, for an exhibition, "Recent Work." Meets Alexander Iolas from Athens, who is a supporter until his death in 1987.

Dedicates a catalog to Amy Plumb, his archivist since 1977.

Builds three permanent outdoor works: *Roots in Cubism. Hearts in the Stars. Forest for Cezanne.,* 1983 at Bundesgarten, Berlin, *Basket and Wave,* 1984-85 at Heide Park and Art Gallery, Melbourne, Australia, and *Levitation, Celebration, Separation.* in Theirs, France.

Buys a house in Springs, near East Hampton, Long Island.

1986
Selected to make the sculpture, *Radiator,* 1983, to top the Charlottenburg Gate, West Berlin, on the occasion of the 750th anniversary of Berlin, although project itself was postponed at a later date.

Joseph Beuys dies of heart failure.

1987
Builds twenty-five prototypes for furniture, called *Functional Stage Sets-Narrative Furniture.*

Andy Warhol dies at fifty-nine years in New York. His estate contains Oppenheim's installation *Theme for a Major Hit.*

1988
Spends the spring in Seoul, Korea, overseeing the fabrication of *Impersonation Station,* an outdoor sculpture for the Olympic Park, commissioned by the Seoul Olympic Organizing Committee. Becomes friends with Jorge DuBon (Mexico), Nigel Helyer (Australia), and Sorel Etrog (Canada), who are among the artists in Seoul.

Jean Baudrillard's *Selected Writings* is published by Stanford University Press, Stanford.

Attends the Olympics with son, Erik.

Travels to Crete for an art symposium, "Contemporary Art and Art Criticism," and to build an outdoor sculpture, *Second Generation Image. Iron/Boat,* with the help of Greek boat builders.

Karen Cackett Dorris, Dennis's first wife, dies in Boise.

1989
Begins a new series of sculptures called the *Power Tools* series.

1990
Installs ten rooms of new sculpture at Ace Contemporary Exhibitions, Los Angeles.

1991
Travels to Porto, Portugal, for an exhibition at the Galeria Pedro Oliveira.

Invited by the Mayor of Madrid to participate with a group of forty international sculptors in the Symposium of International Sculpture in the Open Air.

SELECTED EXHIBITIONS

Selected One-Person Exhibitions

1968
John Gibson Gallery, New York

1969
Galerie Françoise Lambert, Milan
Galerie Yvon Lambert, Paris
John Gibson Gallery, New York

1970
John Gibson Gallery, New York
Reese Palley, San Francisco

1971
Galerie Françoise Lambert, Milan
Galerie Yvon Lambert, Paris

1972
Gallery D, Brussels
Mathias Fels, Paris
Sonnabend Gallery, New York
Tate Gallery, London

1973
Gallery D, Brussels
Gallery Forma, Genoa
Gallery Mayor, London
Museum of Contemporary Art, San Francisco
Sonnabend Gallery, New York
Sonnabend Gallery, Paris

1974
Gallery D, Brussels
Gallery Forma, Genoa
John Gibson Gallery, New York
Oppenheim Studio, Cologne
Paolo Barrozzi, Milan
Stedelijk Museum, Amsterdam

1975
Galerie Yvon Lambert, Paris
Gallery Schema, Florence
Gallery Vega, Liége
John Gibson Gallery, New York
Kitchen Center, New York
Oppenheim Studio, Cologne
Palais des Beaux-Arts, Brussels
P.J.M. Self Gallery, London

1976
Bo Alveryd Gallery, Kavlinge, Sweden
Framartstudio, Naples
M.L.D'Arc Gallery, New York
Museum Boymans van Beuningen,
Rotterdam (retrospective)

1977
Fine Arts Gallery, Wright State
University, Dayton, Ohio
Galerie Hans Mayer, Düsseldorf
Galerie Yvon Lambert, Paris
John Gibson Gallery, New York
M.L.D'Arc Gallery, New York
University of Rhode Island Gallery,
Kingston, Rhode Island

1978
Art Gallery of Ontario, Toronto
(retrospective)
Marian Goodman Gallery, New York
Musée d'Art Contemporain, Montreal
(retrospective)

1979
Galerie Françoise Lambert, Milan
John Gibson Gallery, New York
The Israel Museum, Jerusalem
Kitchen Center, New York
Kunsthalle Basel, Basel
Musée d'Art Moderne de la Ville de
Paris, Paris
Winnipeg Art Gallery, Winnipeg
(retrospective)
Württembergischer Kunstverein
Stuttgart, Stuttgart

1980
Cranbrook Academy of Art, Bloomfield
Hills, Michigan
Flow Ace Gallery, Venice, California
Galerie Yvon Lambert, Paris
Musée d'Art et d'Histoire, Geneva
Portland Center for the Visual Arts,
Portland

1981
The Contemporary Arts Center,
Cincinnati
Galerie Françoise Lambert, Milan
Galerie Marika Malacordia, Geneva
Lowe Art Museum, Miami, Florida
Richard Hines Gallery, Seattle
Sonnabend Gallery, New York

1982
Bonlow Gallery, New York
Galerie Stampa, Basel
Ikon Gallery, Birmingham, England
Lewis Johnstone, London
Musée d'Art et d'Histoire, Geneva
Rijksmuseum Kroller-Muller, Otterlo,
Holland
Vancouver Art Gallery, Vancouver

1983
Akira Ikeda Gallery, Tokyo
Flow Ace Gallery, Venice, California
Galerie Eric Franck, Geneva
Galerie Schurr, Stuttgart
Munson-Willliams-Proctor Institute,
Utica, New York
Seattle Art Museum, Seattle
Whitney Museum of American Art,
New York
Yorkshire Sculpture Park, West Bretton,
England

1984
Braunstein Gallery, San Francisco
Galerie Francoise Lambert, Milan
Galerie Hans Mayer, Düsseldorf
Galerie Yvon Lambert, Paris
La Jolla Museum of Contemporary Art,
La Jolla
Philadelphia Art Alliance, Philadelphia
San Francisco Museum of Modern Art,
San Francisco
Sander Gallery, New York
Tel Aviv Museum, Tel Aviv

1985
Elisabeth Franck Gallery, Knokke,
Belgium
Grand Rapids Art Museum, Grand Rapids
Knight Gallery, Charlotte, North Carolina
Sander Gallery, New York

1986
Laumeier Sculpture Park, St. Louis
Tolarno Galleries, South Yarra, Australia

1988
Anne Plumb Gallery, New York
Walker Hill Art Center, Seoul

1989
Elisabeth Franck Gallery, Knokke,
Belgium
Galerie Yvon Lambert, Paris
John Gibson Gallery, New York
Pace/MacGill Gallery, New York
Paris Art Center, Paris
Anne Plumb Gallery, New York
Willoughby Sharp, New York
Holly Solomon Gallery, New York

1990
Ace Contemporary Exhibitions,
Los Angeles
Dart Gallery, Chicago
Galerie Berndt + Krips, Cologne
Galerie Joachim Becker, Cannes
Galerie Lohrl, Mönchengladbach,
Germany
Galerie Tobias Hirschmann, Frankfurt
John Gibson Gallery, New York
Le Chanjour, Nice
Liverpool Gallery, Brussels
Pierides Museum, Athens

1991
Galerie Friebe, Ludenscheid, Germany
Galerie Gastaud, Clermont-Ferrand,
France
Galeria Pedro Oliveira, Porto, Portugal
Landfall Press, New York

Selected Group Exhibitions

1968
"Earthworks," Dwan Gallery, New York
"Language II-III," Dwan Gallery,
New York
"Sculpture Annual," Whitney Museum
of American Art, New York

1969
"Art After Plans," Berne Kunsthalle,
Berne
"Art by Telephone," Museum of
Contemporary Art, Chicago
"Earth Art," Andrew Dickson White
Museum of Art, Cornell University,
Ithaca
"587-087," Seattle Art Museum, Seattle
"New Media—New Methods," The
Museum of Modern Art, New York
"955,000," Vancouver Art Gallery,
Vancouver
"Op Losse Schtoeven," Stedelijk
Museum, Amsterdam
"Place and Progress," Edmonton Art
Gallery, Edmonton
"Prospect," Stadtische Kunsthalle,
Düsseldorf
"A Report—Two Ocean Projects," The
Museum of Modern Art, New York
"When Attitude Becomes Form," Berne
Kunsthalle, Berne

1970
"Against Order," Institute of
Contemporary Art, Philadelphia
"Arte Povera, Concept Art, Land Art,"
Musee d'Art Moderne, Turin
"Body," Museum of Contemporary Art,
San Francisco
"Information," The Museum of Modern
Art, New York
"Recorded Activities," The Museum of
Modern Art, New York
"Sculpture Annual," Whitney Museum
of American Art, New York
"Situation/Concepts," Taxis Palais
Gallery, Innsbruck, Austria

1971
"Art Systems," Center for Art/
Communication at the Modern Art
Museum of Buenos Aires
"Beyond Law and Order," Stedelijk
Museum, Amsterdam
Biennale, Paris

"Elements," Boston Museum of Fine
 Arts, Boston
"Films/Sonsbeek," Rijksmuseum
 Kroller-Muller, Otterlo, Holland
"Film, Video, Performance," 98 Greene
 Street, New York
"Pier 18," The Museum of Modern Art,
 New York
"Projection '71," Kunsthalle
 Düsseldorf, Düsseldorf
"Sculpture Annual," Whitney Museum
 of American Art, New York

1972
"420 West Broadway," Spoleto Festival,
 Spoleto, Italy
"Thirteen Artists Chosen for
 Documenta," Sonnabend Gallery,
 New York

1973
"Actualite d'un Bilan," Galerie Yvon
 Lambert, Paris
"American Drawings," Whitney
 Museum of American Art, New York

1974
"Art Now," Kennedy Center for the
 Performing Arts, Washington, D.C.
"Instructions," Bruce Gallery, Edinboro
 State University, Edinboro,
 Pennsylvania
"Interventions in Landscape," Mass-
 achusetts Institute of Technology,
 Boston
"112 Greene Street," New York
"Project '74," Kunsthalle Cologne,
 Cologne
"Words and Works," The Institute for
 Art and Urban Resources, The
 Clocktower, New York

1975
"Art as Living Ritual," Vienna
Artpark, Lewiston, New York
"Bodyworks," Museum of
 Contemporary Art, Chicago
"Camera Art," Lunds Konsthall, Lund,
 Sweden
"Labyrinth," Institute of Contemporary
 Art, Philadelphia
"Menace," Museum of Contemporary
 Art, Chicago

1976
"Body Art," Galerie Isy Brachot,
 Brussels
Louisiana Museum of Modern Art,
 Humlebaek, Denmark
"Rooms," The Institute for Art and
 Urban Resources, P.S. 1, Long Island
 City, New York
Venice Biennale, Venice, Italy

1977
"Biennial '77," Whitney Museum of
 American Art, New York
Documenta 6, Kassel, West Germany
"Early Works by Five Contemporary
 Artists," The New Museum, New York
Teheran Museum of Contemporary
 Art, Teheran
"Time," Philadelphia College of Art,
 Philadelphia
"A View of a Decade," Museum of
 Contemporary Art, Chicago
"Wit and Wisdom," Institute of
 Contemporary Art, Boston
"Words," Whitney Museum of
 American Art, New York

1978
"Narrative Art," Contemporary Arts
 Museum, Houston
"Sculpture/Nature," Centre d'Arts
 Plastiques, Bordeaux
"The Sense of Self," Independent
 Curator's Incorporated, Washington,
 D.C.

1979
"Concept, Narrative, Document,"
 Museum of Contemporary Art,
 Chicago
"Dialogue," Akron Art Center, Akron,
 Ohio
"Expansion," Vienna Biennale, Vienna
"Object and Image in Contemporary
 Sculpture," Detroit Institute of Arts,
 Detroit
"Sound," The Institute for Art and
 Urban Resources, P.S. 1, Long Island
 City, New York
"Video Art Symposium," Musée
 National d'Art Moderne, Centre
 Georges Pompidou, Paris

1980
"Architectural Sculpture," Los Angeles
 Institute of Contemporary Art,
 Los Angeles
"Dennis Oppenheim and Les Levine,"
 Marian Goodman Gallery, New York
"Drawings: The Pluralist Decade,"
 Institute of Contemporary Art,
 Philadelphia
"Ecouter pas les Yeux," Musée d'Art
 Moderne de la Ville de Paris, Paris
"Internationale Skulpturen,"
 Wenkenpark, Basel
"Morris, Acconci, Oppenheim,"
 Sonnabend Gallery, New York
ROSC International, Dublin
"Temporal Structures," Wave Hill,
 Riverdale, New York
"The Pluralist Decade," Venice
 Biennale, Venice

1981
"Biennial '81," Whitney Museum of
 American Art, New York
"Machineworks," Institute of
 Contemporary Art, University of
 Pennsylvania, Philadelphia
"Metaphor," Hirshhorn Museum and
 Sculpture Garden, Washington, D. C.
"Myth and Ritual," Kunsthaus Zurich,
 Zurich
"Soundings," Neuberger Museum,
 Purchase, New York
"Video Classics," Bronx Museum,
 Bronx, New York

1982
"Accardi, Oppenheim, Pistoletto,"
 Galerie Mario Pieroni, Rome
"Alea," Musée d'Art Moderne de la
 Ville de Paris, Paris
"Art on the Beach," Creative Time
 Incorporated, New York
"Art Sans Frontières," Galerie Isy
 Brachot, Brussels
"Avanguardia Transavanguardia," Mura
 Aureliane, Rome
Fattoria di Celle, Pistoia, Italy
"Past, Present-Future,"
 Württembergischer Kunstverein
 Stuttgart, Stuttgart

1983
"Kunst mit Photographie,"
 Nationalgalerie Berlin
"Tel-Hai '83," Tel-Hai College Art
 Institute, Upper Galilee, Israel
"Video Art: Retrospectives/
 Perspectives," Palais des Beaux-Arts,
 Brussels

1984
Artpark, Lewiston, New York
"Bruce Nauman/Dennis Oppenheim:
 Drawings and Models for
 Albuquerque Commissions,"
 University Art Museum, University of
 New Mexico, Albuquerque
"Content: A Contemporary Focus,
 1974-1984," Hirshhorn Museum and
 Sculpture Garden, Washington, D.C.
"Land Marks," Edith C. Blum Art
 Institute, Bard College, Annandale-on-
 Hudson, New York

1985
"Installations," Anne Plumb Gallery,
 New York
"The Maximal Implications of the
 Minimal Line," Edith C. Blum Art
 Institute, Bard College, Annandale-on-
 Hudson, New York
"Modern Machines," Whitney Museum
 of American Art at Philip Morris,
 New York

Symposium National de Sculpture
Monumental Metallique, Thiers,
France
"Time: The Fourth Dimension in Art,"
Palais des Beaux-Arts, Brussels

1986
"Fireworks," Butler Institute of
American Art, Youngstown, Ohio
"Television's Impact on Contemporary
Art," Queens Museum, New York

1987
"American Masters: Works on Paper,"
Corcoran Gallery of Art, Washington,
D.C.
"Art That Moves," Laguna Gloria Art
Museum, Laguna, Texas
"This is not a Photograph," John and
Mable Ringling Museum of Art,
Sarasota, Florida

1988
"Contemporary Art and Art Criticism,"
Minos Beach, Crete
"Lost and Found in California," James
Corcoran Gallery, Santa Monica
"Second International Sculpture
Symposium," Olympic Park, Seoul
(American representative)
"Turning Point: Art and Politics in
1968," Cleveland Museum of Art,
Cleveland

1989
"Art in Safe," Mai 36 Galerie, Ruine,
Geneva
"Immaterial Objects," North Carolina
Museum of Art, Raleigh, North
Carolina
"Intuition," John Gibson Gallery,
New York
"Project: Installation," The Aldrich
Museum of Contemporary Art,
Ridgefield, Connecticut

1990
"American Express," John Gibson
Gallery, New York
"Art Conceptuel Formes Conceptual,"
Galerie 1900-2000, Paris
"Casino Fantasma," Casino Municipale
di Venezia, Venice
"Construction in Process: Back in Lodz,
1990," History Museum of Lodz,
Lodz, Poland
"Improbable Machines," Santa Barbara
Museum of Art, Santa Barbara
"Les Quatre Elements," Usine de
Méru, Méru, France
"The Technological Muse," Katonah
Museum of Art, Katonah, New York
"Une Collection Pour La Grande
Arche," La Defense, Paris

1991
"After Duchamp," Galerie 1900-2000,
Paris
"Mechanika," The Contemporary Arts
Center, Cincinnati, Ohio
"Outside America: Going into the
90's," Fay Gold Gallery, Atlanta,
Georgia
"Persona," Oakland Museum, Oakland,
California
"Simposio Internacional de Escultura al
Aire Libre," Madrid, Spain
"Trains: Burden, Kessler, Oppenheim,"
Michael Klein, Inc., New York
"IIIme Biennale de Sculpture," Monte
Carlo, Monaco
"Word as Image," Contemporary Arts
Museum, Houston

PUBLIC COLLECTIONS

Akron Art Museum, Akron
Albright-Knox Art Gallery, Buffalo
Art Gallery of Ontario, Toronto
Art Gallery of Winnipeg, Winnipeg,
Manitoba
Art Institute of Chicago, Chicago
Brainerd Art Gallery, Potsdam, New York
Centre d'Art Plastique Contemporain,
Bordeaux
Corcoran Gallery of Art, Washington,
D.C.
Cranbrook Academy of Art, Bloomfield
Hills, Michigan
Danforth Museum of Art, Framingham,
Massachusetts
Denver Art Museum, Denver
Detroit Institute of Arts, Detroit, Michigan
Edmonton Art Gallery, Edmonton,
Canada
Emanuel Hoffmann-Stiftung, Basel
Everson Museum of Art, Syracuse,
New York
Fattoria di Celle, Pistoia, Italy
Florida Atlantic University, Fort
Lauderdale
F.R.A.C. Nord Pas-de-Calais, France
Grand Rapids Art Museum, Grand
Rapids, Michigan
Haags Gemeentemuseum, Den Haag,
Holland
Herbert F. Johnson Museum of Art,
Ithaca, New York
Indianapolis Museum of Art,
Indianapolis, Indiana
The Institute for Contemporary Art,
P.S. 1 Museum, Long Island City,
New York
Israel Museum, Jerusalem
Kunsthaus Zurich, Zurich

Lannan Foundation, Los Angeles
Laumeier Sculpture Park, St. Louis
Los Angeles County Museum of Art,
Los Angeles
Louisiana Museum of Modern Art,
Humlebaek, Denmark
Milwaukee Art Museum, Milwaukee
Mint Museum, Charlotte, North
Carolina
Munson-Williams-Proctor Institute,
Utica, New York
Musée d'Art et d'Histoire, Geneva
Musée d'Art Moderne de la Ville de
Paris, Paris
Musée National d'Art Moderne, Centre
Georges Pompidou, Paris
Musée de Toulon, Toulon, France
Museum Boymans van Beuningen,
Rotterdam
Museum of Art, Fort Lauderdale
Museum of Contemporary Art, Chicago
Museum of Contemporary Art,
Los Angeles
Museum of Modern Art, New York
Museum van Hedendaagse Kunst,
Ghent, Belgium
National Gallery of Art, Ottawa
Neuberger Museum, Purchase,
New York
Newport Harbor Art Museum,
Newport Beach, California
Oakland Museum, Oakland, California
Pennsylvania Academy of Fine
Arts, Philadelphia
Philadelphia Museum of Art,
Philadelphia
Phoenix Art Museum, Pheonix
Rijksmuseum Kroller-Muller, Otterlo,
Holland
San Diego Museum of Contemporary
Art, La Jolla
San Francisco Museum of Modern
Art, San Francisco
Seattle Art Museum, Seattle
Staatsgalerie Stuttgart, Stuttgart
Stadtischer Museum Abteiberg
Mönchengladbach, Germany
Stedelijk Museum, Amsterdam
Tate Gallery, London
Tel Aviv Museum, Jerusalem
University Art Museum, University of
California, Berkeley
University Art Museum, University of
New Mexico, Albuquerque
University of Alaska, Anchorage
Ville de Thiers, Thiers
Weisman Foundation, Los Angeles
Whitney Museum of American Art,
New York
Worcester Art Museum, Worcester,
Massachusetts

PERMANENT OUTDOOR SCULPTURE

Bundesgarten, Berlin
Roots in Cubism. Hearts in the Stars. Forest for Cezanne.
1983-85

Cranbrook Academy of Art, Bloomfield Hills, Michigan
An Operation for Mining, Elevating, and Converting Underground Memories of a Fifth Season
1980

Fattoria di Celle, Pistoia, Italy
Formula Compound. A Combustion Chamber. An Exorcism (From The Fireworks Series)
1982

Florida Atlantic University, Fort Lauderdale
Woven Explosion (Mondrian Under Pressure)
1983-85

Heide Park and Sculpture Garden, Victoria, Australia
Basket and Wave
1984-85

Indianapolis Museum of Art, Indianapolis
Scan
1982-86

Laumeier Sculpture Park, St. Louis, Missouri
Rolling Explosion
1983-84

Olympic Park, Seoul, Korea
Impersonation Station
1988

Rijksmuseum Kroller-Muller, Otterlo, Holland
Station for Detaining and Blinding Radioactive Horses
1980-82

State University of New York at Potsdam, New York
Formula Compound. A Combustion Chamber. An Exorcism (From The Fireworks Series)
1982-83

Tel-Hai, Upper Galilee, Israel
Dreams and Nightmares. Journey of a Broken Weave (Mondrian Under Pressure)
1983

University of Alaska, Anchorage
Image Intervention
1984

University Art Museum, University of New Mexico, Albuquerque
Dreams and Nightmares. Journey of a Broken Weave (Mondrian Under Pressure)
1981-86

Ville de Thiers, Thiers, France
Levitation, Celebration, Separation
1985

FILM/VIDEO

Often the films and the videotapes that were converted to film were shown on two separate reels, simultaneously projected onto a single wall.

Films
Arm and Asphalt, 1969
Arm and Wire, 1969
Wrist and Land, 1969
Compression—Fern (Face), 1970*
Compression—Fern (Hand), 1970*
Compression—Poison Oak, 1970*
Extended Armor, 1970*
Fusion: Tooth and Nail, 1970*
Glassed Hand, 1970
Ground Mutations (Aspen), 1970
Ground Mutations (Kansas), 1970
Lead Sink for Sebastian, 1970
Leafed Hand, 1970*
Material Interchange, 1970*
Nail Sharpening, 1970*
Parallel Arcs, 1970
Preliminary Test for 65 foot Vertical Penetration, 1970
Pressure Piece (Fingers), 1970*
Pressure Piece (Glass), 1970*
Rocked Hand, 1970*
Rocked Stomach, 1970*
Toward Becoming a Devil, 1970*
Arm Wrestle, 1970-71
Broad Jump, 1970-71
Chrome Fingers, 1971
Compression #1, 1971
Compression #2, 1971
Extended Skin Strata, 1970-71
Foot Pressure, 1970-71
Gingerbread Man, 1970-71*
Landslide #1, 1970-71
Landslide #2, 1970-71
Objectified Counter Forces, 1971
Slow Punch, 1970-71
Stomach X ray, 1970-71
Toward Becoming a Scarecrow, 1971
Disappear, 1972
I'm Failing, 1972
My Father's Socks, 1972
Playing Dead, 1972
Stewing Around, 1972

Brush, 1973
Mittens, 1974
*Compiled as separate film program, "Aspen Projects, 1970-1971."

Videotapes
Nail Sharpening, 1970
Rocked Circle-Fear, 1970
Air Pressure (Face), 1971
Air Pressure (Hand), 1971
Do-It, 1971
Extended Expressions, 1971
Feed-back: Kristin, 1971
A Feedback Situation, 1971
Forming Sounds, 1971
Shadow Project, 1971
Spinal Tap, 1971
Star Exchange, 1971
Two Stage Transfer Drawing (Advancing to a Future State), 1971
Two Stage Transfer Drawing (Returning to a Past State), 1971
Vibration #1, 1971
Vibration #2, 1972
Bar Time, 1975
Drumming up Old Work, 1975
Flash in the Pan, 1975
Pulling, 1975
Spinning Knife, 1975
Spinning a Yarn, 1975
Study, 1975

Film Installations
Film installations often used Technicolor loop projectors.
Material Interchange, 1970
Gingerbread Man, 1970-71
Protection, 1972
Echo, 1973
Whirlpool—Eye of the Storm, 1973

Video Installations
Color Application for Chandra, 1971
Violations, 1971-72
Rehearsal for Five Hour Slump, 1973
Recall, 1974
Black Skin—Black Walls, 1975
Golden Slide Rule, 1975
Mind Twist—Wandering, 1975
Search for Clues, 1976
Untitled Video Installation, 1977
Whipping Into Shape, 1977
Theater Piece, 1978

Installations with 35mm Slide Dissolve System
Ground Gel, 1972
Polarities, 1972
2000' Shadow Projection, 1972

ARTIST'S BOOKS

Flower Arrangement for Bruce Nauman, Multiples, Inc., New York, 1970.
Indentations, Galerie Yaki Kornblit, Amsterdam, 1974.
Proposals 1967-1974, Lebeer-Hossman, Brussels and Hamburg, 1975.

SELECTED BIBLIOGRAPHY

Selected Books and Catalogs

1969

Art Povera, Germano Celant. Praeger Publishers, New York.
Earth Art, Andrew Dickson White Museum of Art, Cornell University, Ithaca.
557,087, Lucy Lippard. Seattle Art Museum, Seattle.
Land Art. Fernsegalerie Gerry Schum, Cologne.
Live in Your Heads: When Attitudes Become Form. Kunsthalle Berne.
Op Losse Schroeven. Stedelijk Museum, Amsterdam.
Prospect '69. Stadtische Kunsthalle Düsseldorf, Düsseldorf.

1971

Art and Life, Ulto Kultermann. Praeger Publishers, New York.
Concept Art, Klaus Honnef. Phaidon Publishers, New York.
Earth, Air, Fire, Water. Boston Museum of Fine Arts, Boston.
Prospect '71: Projection. Art Press Verlag, Düsseldorf.
Situation Concepts. Galerie im Taxi Palais, Innsbruck.
Sonsbeek '71. Sonsbeek Foundation, Arnheim, The Netherlands.
The Structure of Art, Jack Burnham. George Braziller, New York.

1972

Conceptual Art, Ursula Meyer. E.P. Dutton, Publishers, New York.
Il Territorio Magico, Achille Bonita Oliva. Centro di, Florence.
Kunst van de 20e eeuw. Museum Boymans van Beuningen, Rotterdam.
Mathias Fels Exposition. Galerie Mathias Fels, Paris.
Varieties of Visual Experience, Edward Feldman. Prentice-Hall, Inc., Englewood Cliffs, New Jersey and Harry Abrams Publishers. New York.

1973

Actualite d'un Bilan. Galerie Yvon Lambert, Paris.
Aspects de l'Art Actuel. Centro di, Florence.
Man Creates Art Creates Man, Duane Preble. Canfield Press; San Francisco.
Six Years: The Dematerialization of the Art Object, Lucy Lippard. Praeger Publishers. New York.

1974

Art Now. Artrend Foundation, Washington, D.C.
Dennis Oppenheim. Stedelijk Museum, Amsterdam.
Great Western Salt Works, Jack Burnham. George Braziller Publishers, New York.
Images and Icons of the Sixties, Nicolas Calas and Ellen Calas. E.P. Dutton Publishers, New York.
Kunst Bleibt Kunst. Kunsthalle Cologne, Cologne.
Schema Informazione 2. Gallerie Schema, Florence.
Senza Titolo, Germano Celant. Bulzoni Editore, Rome.

1975

American Art of the 20th Century, Sam Hunter. Harry N. Abrams Publishers, New York.
American Sculpture in Process, Wayne Anderson. New York Graphic Society, New York.
Art in Landscape. Independent Curators Incorporated, Washington, D.C.
Art in the World, Stephen Russell. Holt, Rinehart, Winston, Publishers, New York.
Camera Art. Lunds Konsthall, Lund, Sweden.
On ne Regarde pas La Lune, Mais le Dioght qui Montre la Lune. Warwara de la Vaissiere, Paris.
Skira Annuel. Editions Skira S. A., Geneva.
The Tate Gallery. Tate Gallery, London.
Topics in American Art Since 1945, Lawrence Alloway. Norton Publishers, New York.
Video Art. Institute of Contemporary Art, Philadelphia.
Video Art U.S.A. XIII São Paulo Biennale, São Paulo.

1976

Amerikanische Kunst von 1945 bis Heute, Deiter Honisch and Jan Jensen. Dumont Buchverlag, Cologne.
Artpark: The Program in the Visual Arts. Artpark, Lewiston, New York.
Europe/America: The Different Avant-Gardes, Achille Bonita Oliva. Deco Press, New York.
Il Biennale di Venezia (2 vol.). Alfieri Edizioni d'Arte, Venice.
Modern Art and the Object, Ellen Johnson. Harper and Row Publishers, Inc., New York.
Precronistoria 1966-1969, Germano Celant. Centro di, Florence.
Video Art: An Anthology, Ira Scheider and Beryl Korot. Harcourt, Brace and Jovanovich. New York.

1977

Art Now, Edward Lucie Smith. William Morrow and Company, Inc., New York.
Biennial Exhibition. Whitney Museum of American Art, New York.
Early Work by Five Contemporary Artists. The New Museum, New York.
History of Modern Art. H. H. Arneson. Harry Abrams Publishers, New York.
Individuals, Allan Sondheim. E.P. Dutton Publishers, New York.
Rooms. The Institute for Art and Urban Resources, P.S. 1, Long Island City, New York.
A View of a Decade. Museum of Contemporary Art, Chicago.
Why Art, Gregory Battcock. E.P. Dutton Publishers, New York.

1978

Artforms, Duane Preble. Canfield Press, San Francisco.
Artitudes, Francois Pluchart. Galerie de la Marine, Nice.
Dennis Oppenheim: Retrospective Works 1967-1977. Musée d'Art Contemporain, Montreal.
Esthetics Contemporary, Richard Kostelanetz. Prometheus, Buffalo.
New Artists Video, Gregory Battcock. "Video: The Art of Observable Dreams," Mona da Vinci. E. P. Dutton Publishers, New York.
Sculpture/Nature. Centre d'Arts Plastique Contemporains de Bordeaux, Bordeaux.
The Sense of Self. Independent Curators Incorporated, Washington, D.C.
16 Projects/4 Artists. Wright State University, Dayton.

1979

American Art, Sam Hunter. Prentice-Hall, Englewood Cliffs, New Jersey and Harry N. Abrams Publishers, New York.
Dennis Oppenheim. Kunsthalle Basel, Basel.
Dennis Oppenheim. Musée d'Art Moderne de la Ville de Paris, Paris.

Earthworks: Land Reclamation as Sculpture. King County Arts Commission, Seattle.

Image and Object in Contemporary Sculpture. Detroit Institute of Arts, Detroit.

The Writings of Robert Smithson, Nancy Holt. New York University Press, New York.

1980

Architectural Sculpture. (2 vol.) Los Angeles Institute of Contemporary Art, Los Angeles.

The Arts of Twentieth Century America. University Press of America, Lanham, Maryland.

Drawings: The Pluralist Decade. Institute of Contemporary Art, University of Pennsylvania, Philadelphia.

Leben mit Zeitgenossen. Emanual Hoffmann-Stiftung, Basel.

Skulptur in 20. Jahrhundert. Ausstellung in Wenkenpark, Basel.

1981

Art in Our Times, Peter Selz. Harry N. Abrams Publishers, New York.

Biennial Exhibition. Whitney Museum of American Art, New York.

Machineworks. Institute of Contemporary Art, University of Pennsylvania, Philadelphia.

Models and Drawings for Large Scale Sculpture. Richard Hines Gallery, Seattle.

Myth and Ritual. Kunsthaus Zurich, Zurich.

Natur-Skulptur. Württembergischer Kunstverein Stuttgart, Stuttgart.

The Shock of the New, Robert Hughes. Knopf Publishers, New York.

1982

American Artists Talk on Art: From 1940-1980, Ellen Johnson. Harper and Row Publishers, New York.

Avanguardia/Transavanguardia, Achille Bonita Oliva. Gruppo Editorale Electra, Milan.

A Concise History of World Sculpture, Germain Bazin. Alpine Fine Arts Collection, Ltd., New York.

Metaphor: New Projects by Contemporary Sculptors. Hirshhorn Museum and Sculpture Garden, Washington, D.C.

'60-'80: Attitudes/Concepts/Images. Stedelijk Museum, Amsterdam.

1983

Currents: Contemporary Directions in the Visual Arts, Howard Smagula. Prentice-Hall, Inc., Englewood Cliffs, New Jersey.

Dennis Oppenheim. Akira Ikeda Gallery, Tokyo.

Kunst mit Photographie. Die Sammlung Dr. R. H. Krauss, Frolich and Kaufmann, Berlin.

Minimal, Earth and Conceptual Art. Jazzpetie, Prague.

Overlay, Lucy Lippard. Pantheon Books, New York.

Tel-Hai '83, Contemporary Art Meeting. Al Hamishmar, Tel-Aviv.

World Art Trends 1982, Jean Louis Pradel. Harry N. Abrams, Inc., New York.

1984

Bulletin. Allen Memorial Art Museum, Oberlin, Ohio.

Dennis Oppenheim. The Tel Aviv Museum, Helena Rubinstein Pavilion, Tel Aviv.

Land Marks. Edith C. Blum Art Institute, Bard College, Annandale-on-Hudson, New York.

Resource/Reservoir. San Francisco Museum of Modern Art, San Francisco.

1985

Accelerator for Evil Thoughts, Alain Joyaux. Ball State University Art Gallery, Muncie, Indiana.

1988

Dennis Oppenheim. Walker Hill Art Center, Seoul.

1989

Dennis Oppenheim. Elisabeth Franck Gallery, Knokke-Le-Zoute, Belgium.

1990

Dennis Oppenheim. Galerie Lohrl, Mönchengladbach, Germany.

Dennis Oppenheim. Liverpool Gallery, Brussels.

Dennis Oppenheim Retrospective 1970-1990. Pierides Museum of Contemporary Art, Athens.

Selected Periodicals

1968

"The Earth Movers." Time, October 11, p. 84.

Glueck, Grace. "An Artful Summer." The New York Times, May 18, p. D:35.

Hutchinson, Peter. "Earth in Upheaval." Arts, November, pp. 19-21.

Junker, Howard. "Getting Down to the Nitty Gritty." Saturday Evening Post, November 2, pp. 42-47.

———. "The New Art—It's Way, Way Out." Newsweek, July 29, pp. 56-63.

Smithson, Robert. "A Sedimentation of the Mind." Artforum, September, pp. 44-50.

Tillam, Sydney. "Earthworks and the New Picturesque." Artforum, December, pp. 42-45.

1969

"Art You Can Bank On." Life, September, pp. 80-86.

Ashton, Dore. "Exercises in Anti-Style." Arts, April, pp. 45-46.

Borgeaud, Bernard. "Dennis Oppenheim." Pariscope, June 4.

Bourgeois, Jean-Louis. "Dennis Oppenheim: A Presence in the Countryside." Artforum, October, pp. 34-38.

Burnham, Jack. "Real Time Systems," Artforum, September, pp. 49-55.

Celant, Germano. "Nature has Arisen." Casabella, September, pp. 104-07.

Constable, Rosalind. "The New Art—Big Ideas for Sale." New York Magazine, March 10, pp. 80-84.

Glueck, Grace. "Snow Projects from Canadian Borders." The New York Times, June 22, p. 24.

Hahn, Otto. Exhibition review. L'Express, June 2, p. 8.

Hensema, Jan. "Land in Finsterwolde." Winschoter Cournat, April 9, p. 1.

Heubach, Francois. "Land Art/Earth Works." Interfunktionen 3, p. 30.

Perreault, John. "Earth Show." Village Voice, February 27, pp. 16-20.

Sharp, Willoughby. "Place and Progress." Artforum, November, pp. 46-49.

Shirey, David. "Impossible Art—What It Is." Art in America, May, pp. 30-31.

"Televisie Galerie." Museumjournaal, June, pp. 138-40.

Trini, Thomas. "Prodigal Creator's Trilogy," Domus, September, pp. 45-55.

"220 Yard Dash." ArtsCanada, October, pp. 38-39.

1970

"Back to Nature." Time, June 29, pp. 62-65.

Bongartz, Roy. "It's Called Earth Art—and Boulderdash." The New York Times Magazine, February 1, pp. 16-17, 22-30.

Burnham, Jack. "Catalyst 1967-1970." ArtsCanada, August, pp. 42-49.

Calas, Nicolas. "Documentizing." Arts, May, pp. 30-32.

Celant, Germano. "Archives: Dennis Oppenheim." Casabella 46, March, pp. 42-44.

Davis, Douglas. "Art Under Stress." Newsweek, May 25, p. 119.

"Dennis Oppenheim: Decompositions." *Interfunktionen* 4, March, pp. 18-29.

Honnef, Klaus. "Concept Art." *Magazin Kunst,* September, pp. 59-67.

"Kunst als Kontext." *Interfunktionen* 5, pp. 31-41.

"New York." *Domus* 487, June, pp. 49-50.

Sharp, Willoughby. "Discussions with Oppenheim, Heizer, Smithson." *Avalanche* 1, Fall.

1971

Davis, Douglas. "Media/Art/Media." *Art,* September, pp. 43-45.

Kaprow, Allan. "The Education of the Un-Artist (Part I)." *Art News,* February, pp. 28-31, 66-68.

Nemser, Cindy. "Subject-Object: Body Art." *Arts,* September, pp. 38-42.

Pluchart, Francois. "Le Corps, Matericl d'Art." *Artitudes International* 1, October, p. 1-8.

Rabin, Vincente. "Nadie Entiende me Obra Ni Yo Tampoco." *Siete Dias,* October, pp. 50-51.

Schwartz, Ellen. Exhibition review. *Art International,* December 20, p. 80.

"Seht mich an, das Genught." *Der Spiegel,* October 18, pp. 78-79.

Sharp, Willoughby. "A Discussion with Terry Fox, Vito Acconci, and Dennis Oppenheim," *Avalanche* 2, Winter, pp. 18-19.

———. "Interview with Dennis Oppenheim." *Studio International,* November, pp. 183-93.

Tarshis, John. Exhibition review. *Artforum,* February, p. 85.

Venturi, Laura. Exhibition review. *Arts,* March, p. 48.

1972

"Interactions: Form-Energy-Subject." *Arts,* March, pp. 36-39.

Kaprow, Allan. "The Education of the Un-Artist (Part II)." *Art News,* May, pp. 34-39, 62-63.

Matthias, Robert. Exhibition review. *Arts,* November, p. 68.

"Projects 1967-1972." *Interfunktionen* 9, pp. 33-34.

Schwartz, Ellen. Exhibition review. *Art International,* Summer, p. 128.

1973

Baker, Kenneth. Exhibition review. *Art in America,* May, p. 103.

Burnham, Jack. "Artist as Shaman." *Arts,* May/June, pp. 42-44.

Goldberg, Lenore. "Dennis Oppenheim: Myth and Ritual." *Art and Artists,* August, pp. 22-27.

———. "Renewal of Possibilities." *Arts,* November, pp. 42-43.

Hershman, Lynn. "Interview with Dennis Oppenheim." *Studio International,* November, pp. 196-97.

Jochimse, Michel. "Documentation #15." *Magazin Kunst,* January, p. 60.

Lebeer, Irmeline. "Dennis Oppenheim." *Chroniques de l'Art Vivant,* June, pp. 13-15.

———. "Le Corps de l'Oeuvre du Corps." *L'art Vivant,* June, p. 13.

Loring, John. "Open to Re-definition." *Arts,* November, pp. 42-43.

1974

Cameron, Eric. Exhibition review. *Studio International,* December, p. 107.

Driscoll, Ellen. "Back to Nature." *Art News,* September, pp. 80-81.

Jappe, Georg. "Die Unsichtuaren Tiefenschicheen der Energie." *Feuilleton,* April 5, p. 14.

"Performance." *Avalanche,* May/June, p. 4.

Pluchart, François. "Notes sur l'Art Corporel." *Artitudes* 12/14, p. 65.

"Rehearsal for Five Hour Slump." *Art-Rite* 7, Fall, p. 20.

Sharp, Willoughby. "Interview with Dennis Oppenheim." *Magasin Kunst,* January, p. 114.

Smith, Roberta. Exhibition review. *Artforum,* May, p. 71.

Van Tieghem, Jean-Pierre. Exhibition review. *Cles Pour les Arts,* October 4, p. 28.

1975

Baker, Betsy. Exhibition review. *Studio International,* September, p. 164.

Baker, Kenneth. "Dennis Oppenheim: An Art with Nothing to Lose." *Arts,* April, pp. 72-74.

Battcock, Gregory. Exhibition review. *Art and Artists,* June, p. 22.

Bourdon, David. "Far Out and Far In, Uptown and Down." *Village Voice,* January 20, p. 94.

"Dennis Oppenheim." *Arts in Ireland,* June, pp. 46-48

Goldberg, Roselee. "Space as Praxis." *Studio International,* September, p. 132.

Kosloff, Max. Exhibition review. *Artforum,* November, p. 30.

Pluchart, Francois. "L'Art Corporel." *Artitudes International* 18/20, March, pp. 24-27.

Wines, James. "De-Architecturization." *Arts in Society,* Fall/Winter, pp. 351-363.

1976

Braathen, Barbara. "Sport in der Zeitgenossischen Kunst." *Dujournal,* July, pp. 62-63.

Crary, Jonathan. Exhibition review. *Arts,* February, p. 7.

Davis, Douglas. "The Size of Non-Size." December, pp. 46-51.

Derfner, Phyllis. Exhibition review. *Art in America,* May/June, pp. 105-06.

Foote, Nancy. "The Anti-Photographers." *Artforum,* September, pp. 46-54.

———. "Drawing the Line." *Artforum,* May, pp. 54-57.

"I Topi di Oppenheim." *Domus* 556, p. 53.

Kardon, Janet. "Modern Maze Makers." *Art International,* April, p. 66.

Lorber, Robert. Exhibition review. *Arts,* April, p. 19.

Onorato, Ronald. "The Modern Maze." *Art International,* April/May, pp. 21-25.

Russell, John. Exhibition review. *The New York Times,* February 15, p. B:35.

Zandee, Thomas. "Kunstkritiek en de Veelzijde lijfelijkheid van Body Art." *Museumjournaal,* February, pp. 97-106.

1977

Burnside, Madeline. Exhibition review. *Art News,* May, p. 134.

Lippard, Lucy. "Art Outdoors—In and Out of the Public Domain." *Studio International,* February, pp. 83-90.

Onorato, Ronald. "I Shot the Sheriff." *Artforum,* November, pp. 71-72.

Ramsen, Anne. "It Ain't What You Make, It's What Makes You Do It." *Parachute,* Winter, pp. 10-12.

Tatransky, Valentine. Exhibition review. *Arts,* September, p. 21.

1978

Crary, Jonathan. "Dennis Oppenheim's Delirious Operations." *Artforum,* November, pp. 36-40.

Levin, Kim. "Dennis Oppenheim: Post-Performance Works." *Arts,* September, pp. 122-25.

Morgan, Stuart. "Dennis Oppenheim: An Interview." *New York Arts Journal,* November/December, pp. 29-30.

1979

Ammann, Jean-Christophe. "Neue Installationen 1978-1979." *Kunst Magazin,* June, pp. 24-33.

Cuiger, Ben. "Dennis Oppenheim Inder Basler Kunsthalle." *Basler Zeitung,* June 2, p. 26.

Fend, Peter. "Dennis Oppenheim." *Flash Art,* January/February, p. 42

Klepac, Walter. "Conjectural Imaging." *Vanguard,* October, p. 12-16.

Morgan, Stuart. "Gut Reaction." *Artscribe,* February, pp. 34-38.

Reuther, Hans. "Psycho-Installutionen a la Duchamp and Hitchcock." *Feuilleton,* September 10, p. 55.

"Wuste in Lieb." *Der Spiegel,* June 11, p. 183.

1980

"Dennis Oppenheim a l'Arc." *Le Monde,* January 3, p. 11.

Glueck, Grace. Exhibition review. *The New York Times,* January 11, p. C:17.

Larson, Kay. "Metaphysical Attraction." *Village Voice,* March 17, p. 79

Marcelis, Barbara. "Dennis Oppenheim." *Domus* 604, p. 56.

Morgan, Stuart. Exhibition review. *Artforum,* Summer, p. 83.

Poinsot, Jean. Exhibition review. *Artistes,* February/March, p. 40.

Raillard, Georg. "Les Factories de Dennis Oppenheim." *La Quinzaine-littéraire,* January 1, p. 19.

Russell, John. Exhibition review. *The New York Times,* March 21, p. C:21.

Staniszewski, Maryann. Exhibition review. *Art News,* September, p. 248-49.

1981

Braun, Emily. "The Factories." *Arts,* June, pp. 138-41.

Levin, Kim. Exhibition review. *Village Voice,* February 18-24, p. 74.

Morgan, Stuart. Exhibition review. *Artforum,* Summer, pp. 97-98.

Morris, Robert. "American Quartet." *Art in America,* December, p. 69.

Teicher, Hendel. "L'Adventure Dennis Oppenheim à Geneve." *Tribune de geneva,* January 18, pp. 21-25.

Wood, Steve. "An Interview with Dennis Oppenheim." *Arts,* June, pp. 133-37.

1982

Ayers, Robert, "Dennis Oppenheim." *Art Monthly,* May, pp. 17-19.

Larson, Kay. "Apocalypse Now." *New York Magazine,* June 14, pp. 50-54.

Morgan, Stuart. Exhibition review. *Artscribe,* June, pp. 60-62.

Schwartz, Ellen. "Art Between Mind and Matter." *Art News,* December, pp. 56-61.

"Sculpture with a Short Fuse." *Life Magazine,* October, pp. 133-35.

1983

Crary, Jonathan. Exhibition review. *Art in America,* January, p. 87.

Jowett, David. Exhibition review. *Vanguard* 10, January, p. 45.

Robinson, John. "Recent Works of Dennis Oppenheim." *Tableau,* Summer, pp. 406-10.

Walker, Dorothy. "Interview with Dennis Oppenheim." *Studio International* 999, pp. 39-41.

Wall, Donald. "Dennis Oppenheim's Infinitely Ambiguous Objects." *Express,* August/September, p. 8.

1984

Kuspit, Donald. Exhibition review. *Artforum,* December, p. 96.

———. Exhibition review. *Artforum,* May, p. 85.

Lichtenstein, Terry. Exhibition review. *Arts Magazine,* April, p. 71.

Regan Kay. "Sculptor's Factories of Thought." *San Francisco Chronicle,* May 31, p. 64.

1985

Raynor, Vivien. Exhibition review. *The New York Times,* March 15, p. D:34.

Trebay, Guy. "Project Drawings." *Village Voice,* April 2, p. 65.

1986

Harris, John. "Oppenheim Drawings Shown at Laumeier." *St. Louis Post Dispatch,* May 30, p. 48.

1987

"American's Sculpture Will Top West Berlin Gate." *The New York Times,* February 15, p. D:73.

Schultz, Jay. "Eccentric Machines." *New Art Examiner,* September, p. 55.

1988

Kimmelman, Michael. Exhibition review. *The New York Times,* August 19, p. D:33.

Mahoney, Robert. Exhibition review. *New York Press,* August 5, p. 8.

1989

Costa, Vanina. "Dennis Oppenheim." *Beaux-Arts,* March, p. 88.

Crockett, Tobey. "Ghosts in the Machine." *Splash,* February, pp. 80-87.

Izzo, Arcangelo. "The Theatre of Memory." *New Art International,* Summer, pp. 16-23.

Morgan, Robert. Exhibition review. *Arts,* April, p. 96.

Prosperi, Carlo. "Dennis Oppenheim." *New Art International,* Summer, pp. 24-27.

Reid, Calvin. Exhibition review. *Art in America,* July, p. 101.

Rimanelli, David. Exhibition review. *Artforum,* April, p. 89.

Smith, Roberta. "Kinetic Sculpture Using Toys, Fire and Water." *The New York Times,* January 20, p. C:24.

1990

Bloemhard, Marlot. "Dennis Oppenheim." *Tableau,* October, pp. 124-28.

Gilsoul, Guy. "La Mecanique d'Oppenheim." *L'Express,* October 5, p. 165.

McKenna, Kristine. "Cheap Thrills in a Diabolic Realm." *Los Angeles Times,* August 17, p. 79.

Papa, Sania. "Dennis Oppenheim." *Contemporanea,* September, p. 95.

———. "Dennis Oppenheim." *Galeries Magazine,* March, pp. 82-85.

Zahm, Olivier. "Orary Mutations and Trauma." *Diagonals* 1, November/December, pp. 33-37.

1991

"A Conversation with Tricia Collins & Richard Milazzo." *Tema Celeste,* March/April, pp. 68-74.

Crockett, Tobey. "Stalking the Invisible." *Sculpture Magazine,* March/April, pp. 40-47.

"Land Art: Landschaft als Kunst." *Feuilleton,* February 8, p. 8.

The Institute for Contemporary Art

is a nonprofit center for contemporary art committed to the presentation of a broad range of artistic activities in various media through exhibitions, publications, and related activities.

P.S. 1 Museum and The Clocktower Gallery facilities are owned by the City of New York. Their operations are supported in part by the Department of Cultural Affairs, City of New York.

Board of Directors
Anthony M. Solomon, Chairman
Brendan Gill, Chairman Emeritus
Alanna Heiss, President and
  Executive Director
John Comfort, Treasurer
Jane Timken, Secretary

Emilio Ambasz
Richard Bellamy
Kenneth D. Brody
Leo Castelli
Christo
Robert Denison
Edward L. Gardner
Peter A. Gordon
Rita E. Hauser
E. William Judson
Pentti Kouri
Dennis LaBarre
Gianni De Michelis
Claude Picasso
Robert Rauschenberg
Renny Reynolds
Douglas Schoen
Ruth L. Siegel
Sean O. Strub
Enzo Viscusi
Lawrence Douglas Wilder

International Committee
Gianni De Michelis, Chairman
Caresse Lansberg de Alcantara
Leo Castelli
Attilio Codognato
Jack Lang
Doris Lockhart
Claude Picasso
Paolo Sprovieri

The programs of The Institute for Contemporary Art are made possible in part through the generous contributions of the following:
The New York City Department of
  Cultural Affairs
The National Endowment for the Arts
The New York State Council on the Arts

Studio Program Council
The Arts Council of Northern Ireland
Asian Cultural Council
Australia Council
Ireland America Arts Exchange
Fundación Calara, Venezuela
The Irish Arts Council
Korean Culture and Arts Foundation
Ministry of Culture, The Netherlands
Ministry of Foreign Affairs, Norway
NUNSKU, Sweden
Senate for Culture, Berlin
Swiss Ministry of Home Affairs

Corporations
Agip Petroleum Co., Inc.
Barclay's Bank of New York, N.A.
Chase Manhattan Bank, N.A.
Chemical Bank
Citibank, N.A.
Consolidated Edison Company of
  New York
Dime Savings Bank of New York
EniMont Americas Inc.
Girozentrale
Goldman, Sachs and Co.
Houghton Mifflin Company
Istituto Bancario San Paolo di Torino
ITALTEL
Manufacturers Hanover Trust Company
Montedison
Morgan Guaranty Trust Company of
  New York
New York Telephone
Philip Morris Companies Inc.
Pierre Deux Antiques, Inc.
Syntex Corporation (A.M. Solomon)
Time Warner Inc.
Untitled Productions

Foundations
Alcoa Foundation
David Bermant Foundation: Color,
  Light, Motion
The British Council
The Jay Chiat Foundation
Booth Ferris Foundation
Howard Gilman Foundation
Goethe House, New York
Horace W. Goldsmith Foundation
The Greenwall Foundation
Henry J. and Drue E. Heinz Foundation
Jerome Foundation
J.M. Kaplan Fund
The Lannan Foundation
Lemberg Foundation, Inc.
The John D. and Catherine T.
  MacArthur Foundation
The Menemsha Fund
R.D. Merrill Foundation
The New York Community Trust

Bernard Osher Foundation
Pro Helvetia
The Samuel Rubin Foundation
Helena Rubinstein Foundation, Inc.
Lila Wallace-Reader's Digest Fund
The Andy Warhol Foundation for the
  Visual Arts, Inc.

Presidents Council
Carolyn and Kenneth D. Brody
Leo Castelli
Peter A. Gordon
Rita E. Hauser
Ruth and Jerome Siegel
Constance and Anthony M. Solomon

Leadership Council
Christo
Robert Denison
Arlyn and Edward Gardner
Barbara Gladstone
Marian Goodman
Agnes Gund
Ann and Jim Harithas
Edwin Havlovic
Akira Ikeda
E. William Judson
Camille and Dennis LaBarre
H. Charles and Jessie H. Price
Renny Reynolds
Louisa Stude Sarofim
Sean O. Strub
Jane M. Timken

Patrons Council
Richard Bellamy
Joseph Berland
Jane and John Comfort
Paula Cooper
Mr. and Mrs. Kenneth N. Dayton
Mary M. Denison
Laura Donnelley
William S. Ehrlich
Andre Emmerich
Freyda and Ronald Feldman
Howard Gilman
Peggy Hall
Robert Layton
Vera G. List
Ronay and Richard Menschel
Sue and Eugene Mercy, Jr.
David Rockefeller
Mikael and Beth Salovaara
Douglas Schoen
Joyce P. Schwartz
Fredrick Sherman
Jerry I. Speyer
Virginia Wright
Anonymous

Contributing Members

David Bermant
Michael J. Bidlo
Louise Bourgeois
John Chamberlain
Nadar F. Darehshori
Mr. and Mrs. Thomas H. Dittmer
Miner S. and Mary Ann Keeler
Wendy Wilder Larsen
Alfredo de Marzio
James McLaren and Lawton Fitt
Gianni De Michelis
Zachary P. Morfogen
Dorothy E. Moxley
James G. Pepper
Ned L. Pines
George Rickey
Mr. and Mrs. W. M. Roth
Mr. and Mrs. Robert Ryman
Ileana Sonnabend
Robert G. Wilmers
Clark B. Winter, Jr.
Anonymous

Sustaining Members

Bodi
Ruth Bowman
Laura L. Carpenter
Howard M. Cohn
Ana and D. Ronald Daniel
Jacqueline G. Darien
Mr. and Mrs. James S. DeSilva
Robert Djerejian
Sandra Eggers
Carol Eisenberg
Richard Ekstract
Gerald S. Elliott
Mr. and Mrs. Anthony T. Enders
Mr. and Mrs. Philip J. Finkelpearl
Frederick Fischer
Mr. and Mrs. Arthur Fleischer
Arnold and Marie Forde
Bertha H. Friedman
Richard Gluckman
Arthur and Carol Goldberg
Greiner-Maltz Co., Inc.
Joel Hershey and Roy Eddey
Dr. and Mrs. Wallace Bill Kalt
Susan and Howard Kaminsky
Mr. and Mrs. Ira B. Kapp
Burton Kassell
Donald L. Kiel
Alain Kirili and Ariane Lopez-Huici
Edward and Phyliss Kwalwasser
Knight Landesman
Alvin S. Lane
Sydney Lewis
Ellen Liman
Susan Lorence
Curt Marcus
Judith Murray and Robert Yasuda

Judith L. Ostrow
David T. Owsley
Julian Pretto
Mary C. del Rio
Barbara G. Sahlman
Joyce P. Schwartz
Michiyo Shibahara
Kit-Yin Snyder
Horace Solomon
Richard Solomon
Lee R. Stewart
Clara D. Sujo
Van Alst Hardware
Jennifer Vorbach
Mike and Penny Winton
James F. Woodman
Anonymous

Staff

Alanna Heiss, President and
  Executive Director
Anthony Vasconcellos,
  Managing Director
Ryszard Wasko, Program Director
Fraser Mooney, Director of Development
Hank Stahler, Building Director
Carole Kismaric, Director of
  Publications
Zdenka Gabalova, Guest Curator
Rebecca Quaytman, Program
  Coordinator
Tim Noe, Technical Coordinator
Ken Ansley, Fiscal/Systems Manager
Miranda Banks, Publications/Publicity
  Coordinator
Angela Lyras, Executive Assistant
Kathy Kao, Bookkeeper
Fred Cisterna, Assistant
Julie Yee, Assistant
Liz French, Assistant

PICTURE CREDITS

pp. 29-31, 32 (*top*), 36-39, 42-43, 46, 50-52, 54 (*bottom*), 55-57, 60-64, 67, 69 (*bottom*), 70-77, 82-86, 88-91, 102-06, 111, 133 (*top*), 156: Dennis Oppenheim.

p. 10: David Sundberg; p. 11: Salvatore Licitra; p. 19 (*top* and *bottom*): David Sundberg; p. 32 (*bottom left*): David Sundberg; p. 32 (*bottom right*): Stedelijk Museum, Amsterdam; pp. 40-41: Musée d'Art Contemporain, Montreal; p. 45: Shunk-Kender; p. 47: Edmonton Art Gallery, Edmonton; pp. 48-49: Robert R. McElroy, courtesy *Newsweek*; p. 54 (*top*): Reese Palley Gallery, New York; p. 59: Sonnabend Gallery, New York; p. 68 (*top*): Jerry Noe; pp. 78-79: Galerie Francoise Lambert, Milan; pp. 80-81: David Sundberg; p. 87: Musée d'Art Contemporain, Montreal; p. 92: Galerie Yvon Lambert, Paris; p. 93: James de Sana; pp. 94-96: David Schaeter; p. 97: Harry Shunk; pp. 98-99: Framartstudio, Naples; pp. 100-101: Palais des Beaux-Artes, Brussels; p. 107: John Stern; p. 108: Richard Kuster; p. 109: M.L.D'Arc Gallery, New York; p. 110: John Stern; p. 112-15: Earl Ripling; p. 116-17: Israel Museum, Jerusalem; p. 118: Colleen Chartier; p. 119: Werner Schlosket; pp. 120-21: Earl Ripling; p. 122: Françoise Lambert, Milan; p. 123 (*top*): Earl Ripling; p. 123 (*bottom*): Albert V. Vaham Hay; p. 124 (*bottom*): Jim Ball; p. 124 (*top*): Earl Ripling; p. 125 (*top*): André Morain; p. 125 (*bottom*): David Sundberg; pp. 126-27: M.C. Akin; pp. 128-29: Luigi Kurmann; pp. 130-31: Bob Blackwell, courtesy San Francisco Museum of Modern Art; p. 132: Wayne Cozzolino; p. 133 (*bottom*): Kunsthaus, Zurich; pp. 134-35: Art Gallery of Ontario, Toronto; pp. 136, 140-41: Anthony Lesperance; pp. 142-43 Henry Groskinsky; p. 144: David Sundberg; p. 148: Ace Contemporary Exhibitions, Los Angeles; p. 149: Artpark, Lewiston, New York; p. 159-60: Ace Contemporary Exhibitions, Los Angeles; p. 165: Anne Plumb Gallery, New York; p. 166: Ace Contemporary Exhibitions, Los Angeles; p. 167 (*bottom left*): Angela Kumerbirch; pp. 168-69,: Ace Contemporary Exhibitions, Los Angeles; pp. 171, 173: Ace Contemporary Exhibitions, Los Angeles; p. 175: David Sundberg; pp. 176-77, 180; p. 181: Galerie Pedro Oliveira, Porto, Portugal.